A History of the 38th (Welsh) Division

A History of the 38th (Welsh) Division

By the G.S.O's.I of the Division.

Edited by Lieut.-Colonel J. E. Munby,

C.M.G., D.S.O.

The proceeds of the sale of this History are devoted to the Welsh Headquarters of the Comrades of the Great War Association.

London :

HUGH REES, Ltd.

5 AND 7, REGENT STREET

1920

Printed & bound by Antony Rowe Ltd, Eastbourne

TABLE OF CONTENTS.

INTRODUCTION

By *Field-Marshal Earl Haig*, *K.T.*, *G.C.B.*, *O.M.*, *G.C.V.O.*, *K.C.I.E.*, *C.-in-C.*

G.H.Q. THE FORCES IN GREAT BRITAIN,
HORSE GUARDS,
LONDON, S.W. 1.

26th November, 1919.

I do not think that there is any Division which fought under my command in France which cannot point to at least one occasion when its actions reached the highest level of soldierly achievement. Those who read through the pages of this book may find several occasions, but two come immediately to my mind. The one is the attack north of Ypres on the 31st July, 1917, when the 38th (Welsh) Division met and broke to pieces a German Guard Division.

The other is that of the operation against Pozieres on the 21st-24th August, 1918—a most brilliant operation alike in conception and execution which, with the days of heavy but successful fighting that followed it, was of very material assistance to our general advance.

To both occasions, all who fought with the 38th Division can look back with legitimate pride.

(Sd.) HAIG,
Field-Marshal.

ORDER OF BATTLE.

38TH (WELSH) DIVISION.

"D" Squadron, Royal Wiltshire Yeomanry. — Joined the Division at Winchester. Withdrawn from the Division to rejoin the Regiment, May, 1916.

119th Brigade, R.F.A. — Withdrawn from the Division and transformed into an Army Field Artillery Brigade, January, 1917.

120th Brigade, R.F.A. — Disbanded, October, 1916, on the augmentation of batteries to six guns.

121st Brigade, R.F.A.
122nd Brigade, R.F.A.
38th Heavy Battery. — Withdrawn from the Division before the latter moved to Winchester.

Divisional Ammunition Column.
(a) "V" Trench Mortar Battery (Heavy). — Organised, January, 1916. Withdrawn from the Division, Feb., 1918.
(b) "X" ,, ,, ,, (Medium). — Organised, January, 1916.
(c) "Y" ,, ,, ,, — Organised, January, 1916.
(d) "Z" ,, ,, ,, — Organised, January, 1916. Disbanded, Feb., 1918, on augmentation of "X" and "Y."

123rd Field Company, R.E.
124th Field Company, R.E.
151st Field Company, R.E.
Divisional Signal Company.
113th Infantry Brigade.
13th Batt. Royal Welsh Fusiliers.
14th Batt. ,, ,, ,,
15th Batt. ,, ,, ,, (The London Welsh).
16th Batt. ,, ,, ,,
113th Machine Gun Company. — Disbanded February, 1918.

113th Light Trench Mortar Battery. — Organised April, 1916. Became "A" Coy., 38th Batt. Machine Gun Corps, March, 1918. Formed May, 1915, but not officially organised till January, 1916.

114th Infantry Brigade.
- (a) 10th (1st Rhondda) Batt. The Welsh Regt.
- (b) 13th (2nd Rhondda) ,, ,, ,, ,,
- (c) 14th (Swansea) ,, ,, ,, ,,
- (d) 15th (Carmar'shire) ,, ,, ,, ,,

114th Machine Gun Company. — Organised April, 1916. Became "B" Coy. 38th Batt., M.G.C., March, 1918.

114th Light Trench Mortar Battery. — Formed May, 1915, but not officially organised till January, 1916.

115th Infantry Brigade. — Joined the Division 6th February, 1918.
- (a) 2nd Batt. Royal Welsh Fusiliers.
- (b) 17th Batt. ,, ,, ,, — Disbanded February, 1918.
- (c) 10th (1st Gwent) Batt. South Wales Bord's — Disbanded February, 1918.
- (d) 11th (2nd Gwent) Batt. ,, ,, ,,
- (e) 16th (Cardiff City) Batt. The Welsh Regt.

115th Machine Gun Company. — Organised April, 1916. Became "C" Coy. 38th Batt., M.G.C., in March, 1918.

115th Light Trench Mortar Battery. — Formed May, 1915, but not officially organised till January, 1916.

19th (Glamorgan Pioneer) Batt. The Welsh Regt.

Divisional Cyclist Company. — Withdrawn from the Division May, 1917, and incorporated in the 11th Corps' Cyclist Battalion.

Machine Gun Battalion. — Organised March, 1918.

176th Machine Gun Company. — Joined the Division from the Grantham Training Centre and Aldershot, March, 1917. Became "D" Coy. 38th Batt., M.G.C., March, 1918.

Divisional Train (Nos. 330–333 Companies, A.S.C.)

129th Field Ambulance.

130th (St. John) Field Ambulance.

131st Field Ambulance.

No. 5 Mobile Bacteriological Section. — Withdrawn from the Division on its arrival in France.

49th Mobile Veterinary Section.

235th Divisional Employment Company. — Formed March, 1917.

38th Divisional Mechanical Transport Company. — Joined the Division December, 1915.

ROLL OF COMMANDERS AND STAFF.

DIVISION— Major-General Sir Ivor Phillips, K.C.B., D.S.O.
                 Jan., 1915.
     Major-General C. G. Blackader, C.B., D.S.O., A.D.C.
                 July, 1916.
     Major-General T. A. Cubitt, C.B., C.M.G., D.S.O.
                 May, 1918.

STAFF.

G.S.O. 1.	Lieut.-Colonel H. E. ap Rhys Pryce, C.M.G., D.S.O.	June, 1915.
	Lieut.-Colonel J. E. Munby, C.M.G., D.S.O.	Oct., 1917.
G.S.O. 2.	Major H. C. Rees, D.S.O.	July, 1915.
	Capt. A. Smith, M.C.	July, 1916.
	Major R. S. Follett, D.S.O.	May, 1917.
	Capt. B. C. Tower, M.C.	Jan., 1918.
	Major Tallents, D.S.O.	Feb., 1918.
	Major M. H. King, M.C.	Aug., 1918.
G.S.O. 3.	Capt. P. R. M. Alexander	Dec., 1915.
	Capt. W. Garforth	June, 1916.
	Capt. G. Drake-Brockman, M.C.	July, 1916.
	Capt. F. J. Harington, D.S.O.	May, 1917.
	Capt. A. Vernon-Jones	Sept., 1918.
A.A. & Q.M.G.	Lieut.-Colonel H. E. ap Rhys Pryce, C.M.G., D.S.O.	April, 1915.
	Lieut.-Colonel C. E. Willes	Sept., 1915.
	Lieut.-Colonel H. M. Pryce-Jones, D.S.O., M.V.O., M.C.	Sept., 1915.
	Lieut.-Colonel H. R. Lee, C.M.G., D.S.O.	Dec., 1917.
D.A.A.G.	Major H. M. Pryce-Jones, D.S.O., M.V.O., M.C.	
	Major Sir G. D. S. Dunbar	
	Major H. R. Lee, C.M.G., D.S.O.	Dec., 1916.
	Major A. H. B. Foster, D.S.O.	Dec., 1917.
	Major S. A. Thompson	June, 1918.
	Major J. R. Graystone, M.C.	Nov., 1918.
	Major A. O. Cushny, M.C.	Dec., 1918.
D.A.Q.M.G.	Major B. A. C. Teeling,	Feb., 1916.
	Major H. M. Jackson	Feb., 1917.
	Major Eardly Wilmot	March, 1918.
	Major H. Davies, M.C.	March, 1918.
	Major N. S. Bostock, M.C.	July, 1918.

ARTILLERY.

C.R.A.	Brig.-General W. A. M. Thompson, C.B., C.M.G.	July, 1915.
	Brig.-General T. E. Topping, C.B., C.M.G., D.S.O.	April, 1918.

119*th Brigade*—
Lieut.-Colonel P. J. Paterson, D.S.O.　　Nov., 1915.

120*th Brigade*—
Lieut.-Colonel C. O. Head　　May, 1915.

121*st Brigade*—
Lieut.-Colonel F. A. Tighe　　July, 1915.
Lieut.-Colonel H. G. Pringle, D.S.O.　　Nov., 1915.
Lieut.-Colonel G. P. Macclellan, D.S.O. March, 1917.

122*nd Brigade*—
Lieut.-Colonel J. Gardner　　Feb., 1915.
Lieut.-Colonel W. C. E. Rudkin, C.M.G., D.S.O.　　Nov., 1915.
Lieut.-Colonel R. C. Williams, D.S.O.　　April, 1918.

38*th D.A.C.*—
Lieut.-Colonel G. W. Hayward, D.S.O.　July, 1915.
　　C.R.E. Colonel Pearson　　Nov., 1914.
Lieut.-Colonel E. H. de Vere Atkinson, C.B., C.M.G.
　　C.I.E.　　Aug., 1915.
Lieut.-Colonel G. C. Falcon, D.S.O.　　July, 1916.
Lieut.-Colonel B. S. Phillpots, D.S.O.　　Oct., 1916.
Lieut.-Colonel T. E. Kelsall, D.S.O.　　Sept., 1917.

113TH BRIGADE—

Brigadiers. Brig.-General Owen Thomas, M.P.　　Oct., 1914.
Brig.-General L. A. E. Price-Davies, V.C., C.M.G., D.S.O.　　Nov., 1915.
Brig.-General H. E. ap Rhys Pryce, C.M.G., D.S.O.　　Nov., 1917.
Brig.-General A. Carton de Wiart, V.C., C.M.G., D.S.O.　　Nov., 1918.
Bgde. Majors. Major C. S. Flower　　Sept., 1914.
Capt. R. Bently　　Oct., 1915.
Capt. J. C. McD. Stewart　　Aug., 1916.
Capt. L. B. Brierley, M.C.　　May, 1917.
Capt. M. G. Richards, M.C.　　Jan., 1918.
13*th R.W.F.*—
Lieut.-Colonel Dunn　　Oct., 1914.
Lieut.-Colonel Willes　　Dec., 1914.
Lieut.-Colonel Flower　　Oct., 1915.
Lieut.-Colonel Campbell, D.S.O.　　July, 1916.
Lieut.-Colonel Leman, D.S.O.　　Nov., 1917.

113TH BRIGADE—*continued*

14*th R.W.F.*—

Lieut.-Colonel David-Davies, M.P.	Nov., 1914.
Lieut.-Colonel H. V. R. Hodson	July, 1916.
Lieut.-Colonel E. W. P. Unlacke, D.S.O.	June, 1917.
Lieut.-Colonel B. W. Collier, D.S.O.	March, 1918.
Lieut.-Colonel C. C. Norman, D.S.O.	Nov., 1918.

15*th R.W.F.* (*The London Welsh*)—

Lieut.-Colonel Fox-Pitt	Nov., 1914.
Lieut.-Colonel J. C. Bell, D.S.O.	
Lieut.-Colonel C. C. Norman, D.S.O.	
Lieut.-Colonel R. H. Montgomery	

16*th R.W.F.*—

Lieut.-Colonel Wynne-Edwards	Dec., 1915.
Lieut.-Colonel R. J. Carden	Nov., 1915.
Lieut.-Colonel A. N. G. Jones, D.S.O.	July, 1916.
Lieut.-Colonel H. F. N. Jourdain, C.M.G.	June, 1917.
Lieut.-Colonel E. J. de P. O'Kelly, D.S.O.	Nov., 1917.
Lieut.-Colonel C. E. Davies, D.S.O.	July, 1918.

114TH BRIGADE—

Brigadiers.	Brig.-General R. H. W. Dunn	Oct., 1914.
	Brig.-General T. O. Marden, C.B., C.M.G., D.S.O.	Dec., 1915.
	Brig.-General A. Harman, C.M.G., D.S.O.	Aug., 1917.
	Brig.-General T. Rose Price, C.M.G., D.S.O.	Aug., 1918.
Bgde. Majors.	Major Umpfreville	March, 1915.
	Capt. C. H. R. Crawshay	Dec., 1915.
	Major A. P. Bowen, M.C.	June, 1916.
	Major F. M. Nixon	Feb., 1917.
	Capt. G. C. Bucknall, M.C.	June, 1917.

10*th* (1*st Rhondda Batt.*) *The Welsh Regiment*—

Lieut.-Colonel Holloway	Oct., 1914.
Lieut.-Colonel P. E. Ricketts, M.V.O.	Dec., 1915.
Lieut.-Colonel G. F. Brooke, D.S.O.	Aug., 1916.

13*th* (2*nd Rhondda Batt.*) *Welsh Regiment*—

Colonel Sir W. Watts, K.C.B.	Nov., 1914.
Lieut.-Colonel Gifford	June, 1915.
Lieut.-Colonel F. E. Packe	March, 1916.
Lieut.-Colonel J. Kennedy, D.S.O., M.C., D.C.M.	July, 1916.
Lieut.-Colonel H. F. Hobbs, D.S.O., M.C.	Oct., 1918.

114TH BRIGADE—*continued.*

14th (*Swansea*) *Batt., The Welsh Regiment*—

Lieut.-Colonel H. W. Benson, D.S.O.	Sept., 1914.
Lieut.-Colonel L. R. King	Dec., 1915.
Lieut.-Colonel J. H. Hayes, D S.O.	April, 1916.
Lieut.-Colonel G. F. Brooke, D.S.O.	Jan., 1918.

15th (*Carmarthenshire*) *Batt., The Welsh Regiment*—

Lieut.-Colonel Scobie, C.B.	Oct., 1914·
Lieut.-Colonel T. W. Parkinson, D.S.O.	Nov., 1915·

115TH BRIGADE—

Brigadiers.

Brig.-General H. J. Evans	Dec., 1915.
Brig.-General C. J. Hickie	Aug., 1916.
Brig.-General J. R. M. Minshall Ford, D.S.O.	
	March, 1917.
Brig.-General H. Cope, D.S.O.	
Brig.-General G. Gwyn Thomas, C.M.G., D.S.O.	
	July, 1917.
Brig.-General W. B. Hulke, D.S.O.	April, 1918.
Brig.-General H. D. de Pree, C.B., C.M.G.	
	Sept., 1918·

Bgde. Majors.

Capt. C. L. Veal	Dec., 1915·
Major A. Derry	July, 1916.
Major V. C. Bawdon, D.S.O.	March, 1917.
Capt. M. H. King, M.C.	July, 1917.
Capt. A. V. Wright, M.C.	Aug., 1918.

2nd *R.W.F.*—

Lieut.-Colonel W. B. Garnett, D.S.O.	March, 1917.
Lieut.-Colonel G. E. de Miremont, D.S.O., M.C.	
	May, 1918.
Lieut.-Colonel J. B. Cockburn, D.S.O.	Aug., 1918.

17th *R.W.F.*—

Colonel H. R. H. Lloyd Mostyn	March, 1915.
Lieut.-Colonel J. A. Ballad	Dec., 1915.
Lieut.-Colonel J. B. Cockburn, D.S.O.	July, 1916.
Lieut.-Colonel H. J. Taylor, D.S.O.	Nov., 1916.
Lieut.-Colonel Cockburn, D.S.O.	Aug., 1917.
Lieut.-Colonel C. C. Norman, D.S.O.	July, 1918.
Lieut.-Colonel R. L. Beasley, D.S.O.	Sept., 1918.

10th (*1st Gwent*) *Batt., S.W.B.*—

Lieut.-Colonel Sir Hamar Greenwood, Bt., M.P.	
	Nov., 1914.
Lieut.-Colonel J. S. Wilkinson, D.S.O.	April, 1916.
Lieut.-Colonel C. D. Harvey, D.S.O.	July, 1916.

115TH BRIGADE—*continued.*

11th (2nd Gwent) Batt., S.W.B.—

    Lieut.-Colonel H. E. Porter   Dec., 1914.

    Lieut.-Colonel J. R. Gaussen, C.M.G., D.S.O.

        March, 1917.

    Lieut.-Colonel A. H. Radice

    Major T. H. Morgan

16th Welsh (Cardiff City)—

    Lieut.-Colonel Gaskel

    Lieut.-Colonel F. W. Smith   May, 1916.

19th Welsh Regiment (Glamorgan Pioneers)—

    Major J. Owen James   March, 1915.

    Lieut.-Colonel D. Grant-Dalton, C.M.G., D.S.O.

        April, 1916.

    Lieut.-Colonel S. J. Wilkinson, D.S.O. Nov., 1915.

    Lieut.-Colonel R. B. Harkness   Oct., 1918.

38th Batt., M.G.C.—

    Lieut.-Colonel A. G. Lyttelton, D.S.O. Feb., 1918.

38th Divisional Train—

    Lieut.-Colonel H. E. Sykes   Feb., 1915.

    Lieut.-Colonel H. F. T. Fisher   June, 1915.

    Lieut.-Colonel T. E. Bennett, D.S.O., O.B.E.

        March, 1916.

A.D.M.S.—

    Colonel F. J. Morgan, C.M.G.   Jan., 1915.

    Colonel J. G. Gill, D.S.O.   Feb., 1917.

    Colonel A. G. Thompson, C.M.G., D.S.O. June, 1917.

129th Field Ambulance—

    Lieut.-Colonel R. J. Simons   March, 1915.

    Lieut.-Colonel W. G. Edwards   Aug., 1915.

    Lieut.-Colonel A. Jones, D.S.O., M.C. July, 1917.

    Lieut.-Colonel A. H. T. Davis   Nov., 1918.

130th Field Ambulance—

    Lieut.-Colonel J. E. H. Davies, D.S.O.

131st Field Ambulance—

    Lieut.-Colonel W. P. Gwynne   March, 1915.

    Lieut.-Colonel R. H. Mills-Roberts, C.M.G.

        April, 1915.

    Lieut.-Colonel J. C. Sproule   Feb., 1918.

A History of the 38th (Welsh) Division.

CHAPTER I

FORMATION OF THE DIVISION.

On the 28th September, 1914, a representative meeting of all classes of the Principality of Wales was held at Cardiff where Mr. Lloyd George, then Chancellor of the Exchequer explained the aims of forming a Welsh Army Corps.

On the 10th October the following letter was addressed by the Army Council to the G.O.C. in command of Western Command.

" I am commanded by the Army Council to inform you that sanction is given to raise the necessary troops in Wales and Monmouthshire and from Welshmen resident in London, Liverpool and Manchester to form a Welsh Army Corps consisting of two divisions . . . The Infantry battalions will be service battalions of the Royal Welsh Fusiliers, South Wales Borderers, and Welsh Regiment."

But it will be seen that the motive power which was responsible for the birth of the Welsh Division was a spontaneous desire on the part of the people of Wales to take part in the Great War and the meeting alluded to above was the result and not the cause of this desire, for several of the units which later comprised the Division had already sprung into being.

B

INFANTRY.

Dealing first with the Infantry whose movements are more easy to follow and taking each Brigade in numerical order we find that the Infantry Brigades were at first numbered the 128th, 129th and 130th Brigades of the 43rd Division (1st Division Welsh Army Corps).

On the 3rd September the War Office sanctioned the raising of a North Wales' " Pals " Battalion of the Royal Welsh Fusiliers and sixty-eight recruits joined and formed the nucleus of that battalion at Rhyl on the 2nd October.

On the 30th October Lieut.-Col. Owen Thomas was appointed to command the 128th Brigade and on the 2nd November he commenced raising a Carnarvon and Anglesey Battalion at Llandudno which had its headquarters at Maenan House, Lloyd Street, and became the 14th Battalion Royal Welsh Fusiliers.

On the 18th November the " Pals " Battalion joined the Brigade at Llandudno from Rhyl and became the 13th Royal Welsh Fusiliers and by that time the recruiting had become so brisk that the Battalion was over strength and sanction was obtained to form a 16th Battalion ; consequently all officers and men surplus to the establishment of the 13th became the 16th Battalion. The number 16 was allotted to this Battalion because the 15th Battalion already existed in London.

This latter was first inaugurated at a meeting of Welshmen in London on September 16th, presided over by Sir E. Vincent Evans, and recruits began to pour in ; but it was not until October 29th that the Battalion was officially recognised and in the meantime many of the recruits were unable to remain quiet and joined other regiments ; the remainder however were kept together by the London Committee but continued to live in their own homes ; the Headquarters of the Battalion was at the Inns of Court

Hotel, Holborn, and the Benchers of Gray's Inn lent the Gardens and Squares as drill grounds. The Battalion joined the Brigade at Llandudno on the 5th December.

The history of the formation of the 114th Brigade shows more variety of dates and places.

The 10th Battalion was recruited in the Rhondda Valley and was formed on October 1st at Codford St. Mary in Wiltshire as part of the 25th Division but on the 30th of that month the Battalion was transferred to the 129th Brigade of the 43rd Welsh Division at Rhyl and became the 10th Battalion (1st Rhondda) The Welsh Regiment and now numbered six officers and 800 other ranks.

The 13th Battalion was recruited from the same district and formed at Sophia Gardens, Cardiff, on October 23rd, though the elements of the Battalion had been forming prior to that date at the Depot Barracks, Cardiff, and by that time the Battalion was 500 strong.

On the 3rd November the Battalion moved to Prestatyn and on the 17th joined the 129th Brigade at Rhyl and became the 13th Battalion (2nd Rhondda) The Welsh Regiment.

The 14th Battalion had its origin in the Swansea Cricket and Football Club who formed a Club Training Corps on August 13th and turned part of the grounds into a rifle range ; the Corps was subsequently adopted by the Township ; a subscription of £7000 was raised for its maintenance, by the end of September 200 men had been enrolled and drill was in full swing on the Swansea Cricket Field.

The Battalion joined the 129th Brigade at Rhyl on the 1st of December and became the 14th (Swansea Battalion) The Welsh Regiment.

The formation of the 15th Battalion bears a later date and the nucleus of the Battalion was made at Rhyl by a draft of seventy-one men (mostly from Lancashire) from the 10th Battalion on the 21st November. A draft of 350 joined the Battalion on January 23rd from Porthcawl,

250 men were enlisted in Lancashire (chiefly from the Bolton district) and it was not until the end of February that the Battalion was made up to full strength by men enlisted in Carmarthenshire.

The Battalion took its place in the 129th Brigade as the 15th (Carmarthenshire Battalion) The Welsh Regiment.

The whole of the 115th Brigade is of a later origin.

The 10th S.W.B. commenced recruiting on the 12th November at Ebbw Vale and Cwm and drew recruits from Tredegar, Abercarn, Crumlin, Pontnewydd, Newport, Blackwood and Abertillery ; those recruits were almost entirely composed of Monmouthshire colliers and iron-workers. By the 4th December the strength of the Battalion was 320, and on the 30th December it moved to Colwyn Bay nearly 600 strong to join the 130th Brigade as the 10th Battalion (1st Gwent) South Wales Borderers and not till then were they organised in four companies.

The 11th S.W.B. was formed on December 5th at the depot at Brecon and on January 9th joined the 130th Brigade at Old Colwyn only 100 strong. Recruiting was carried out in the Gwent district of Monmouthshire and Breconshire and especially at Pengam, and at first was slow ; but later became so brisk that both the 10th and 11th Battalions each sent a company to form part of the 13th Battalion. Some 100 recruits were enlisted in Liverpool. The Battalion was named the 11th Battalion (2nd Gwent) South Wales Borderers.

The 17th R.W.F. with the 18th and 19th Battalions of that Regiment was originally formed on the 2nd February as part of the 128th Brigade. The headquarters of the Battalion was at Charlton Street, Llandudno, and a recruiting depot was formed at Blaenaw Festiniog. The Battalion remained with this Brigade till the 14th July, 1915, when it was transferred to the 130th Brigade (by that time renumbered 115).

The 16th (Cardiff City) Battalion Welsh Regiment commenced recruiting in November, 1914, in Cardiff and owed its origin to the Cardiff City Council. The Battalion was however actually formed at Porthcawl and moved from there to join the 130th Brigade at Colwyn Bay, on 31st December, 1914, being at that time 500 strong. The Battalion was authorised by the War Office to wear the Cardiff City coat of arms as their badge.

The 19th Welsh were formed as the Divisional Pioneer Battalion at Colwyn Bay in February, 1915, and the nucleus of the Battalion was composed of drafts from infantry battalions of the Division but the majority of the men were recruited direct from Glamorganshire, hence the title of the Battalion " Glamorgan Pioneers " ; in April drafts were received from the 123rd and 151st Field Coys., R.E. The Battalion was with Divisional Headquarters at Colwyn Bay until the move to Winchester. It is believed that the Battalion was the first Pioneer Battalion to be enlisted as such.

On the 29th April, 1915, the number of the Division was changed to 38th, and the Brigades were renumbered 113th, 114th and 115th.

About this time the idea of forming a Welsh Army Corps of Service Battalions was abandoned and the 38th Division became known as the Welsh Division.

The Headquarters of the Division (then the 43rd) were first established at Colwyn Bay on the 19th January.

By the end of October, 1914, there had collected at Sophia Gardens, Cardiff, several thousand recruits for the Welsh Division.

Among these the only formed bodies which existed at that time were one battery of Field Artillery (later to become A/120), The 13th (Rhondda) Battalion. The Welsh Regiment and the 2nd (St. John) Field Ambulance. A great sorting out then took place and all men found suitable as Artillery, Engineers or A.S.C. were sent to

Porthcawl while those for the Infantry either left for
Prestatyn with the 13th Welsh or were sent as drafts to
the 14th and 15th Welsh at Rhyl.

ARTILLERY.

All recruits for the Artillery remained at Porthcawl
formed into subsections only and were not formed into
batteries till the beginning of January. At the beginning
of February the four batteries which had been formed
were numbered one to four and sent off to Pwllheli. Then
at dates varying from ten days to six weeks later these
four batteries were each ordered to form a second battery ;
there were thus four pairs of batteries and each of these
eight batteries was eventually divided into two, thus
making the sixteen batteries of the Divisional Artillery,
each brigade being descended from one of the original four
batteries.

But this simple system of expansion was not contemplated from the first ; at one time when the twin batteries
Nos. 3 and 7 moved to Criccieth they were accompanied
by No. 8 and the whole were designated the " Fourth Temporary Brigade 43rd Divisional Artillery."

The genealogical tree shown below will explain the
birth and origin of the eventual batteries. The places and
dates given are the birthplaces and birthdays of the batteries.

The only battery that claims an organised existence as
such prior to February is A/120 which was formed at
Sophia Park Gardens, Cardiff, towards the end of October
and went from there with the remainder of the Artillery
recruits to the training camp at Porthcawl and left there
in February as No. 1 Battery.

The need of equipment was felt even more by the Artillery
than by other arms and gun drill had to be carried out

with improvised weapons such as a pair of old 'bus wheels fitted with a pole and hook (so that limbering-up could be practised).

Half the Artillery remained at Pwllheli until the move to Winchester and they testify to the kindness of Mr. Solomon Andrews and the Township in lending the Recreation Ground as a drill field.

Horses for all batteries began to arrive (in very small numbers) in April and it was decided to horse C/121st Battery with all the greys and roans ; these horses stayed with that battery until just before the battle of the Somme, 1916, when they were exchanged (at St. Pol) for bays and browns from the D.A.C. The greys were a feature of the D.A.C. till the end.

No. 1.

Pwllheli, 1/2/1915.

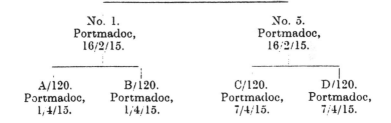

No. 1. Portmadoc, 16/2/15.		No. 5. Portmadoc, 16/2/15.	
A/120. Portmadoc, 1/4/15.	B/120. Portmadoc, 1/4/15.	C/120. Portmadoc, 7/4/15.	D/120. Portmadoc, 7/4/15.

No. 2.

Pwllheli, 3/2/1915.

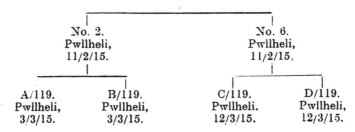

No. 2. Pwllheli, 11/2/15.		No. 6. Pwllheli, 11/2/15.	
A/119. Pwllheli, 3/3/15.	B/119. Pwllheli, 3/3/15.	C/119. Pwllheli. 12/3/15.	D/119. Pwllheli, 12/3/15.

No. 3.

Pwllheli, 3/2/15.

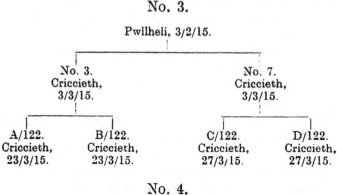

No. 3.
Criccieth,
3/3/15.

No. 7.
Criccieth,
3/3/15.

A/122.
Criccieth,
23/3/15.

B/122.
Criccieth,
23/3/15.

C/122.
Criccieth,
27/3/15.

D/122.
Criccieth,
27/3/15.

No. 4.

Pwllheli, 3/2/1915.

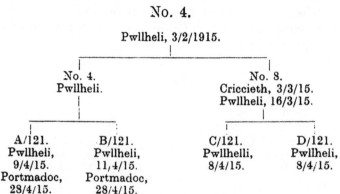

No. 4.
Pwllheli.

No. 8.
Criccieth, 3/3/15.
Pwllheli, 16/3/15.

A/121.
Pwllheli,
9/4/15.
Portmadoc,
28/4/15.

B/121.
Pwllheli,
11/4/15.
Portmadoc,
28/4/15.

C/121.
Pwllhelli,
8/4/15.

D/121.
Pwllheli,
8/4/15.

ROYAL ENGINEERS.

Both the 123rd and 124th Field Coys., R.E. originated from the 13th (Rhondda Battalion) The Welsh Regiment who were being organised at Sophia Gardens, Cardiff. It was found that this Battalion included among its numbers a large percentage of skilled craftsmen and 650 of these men were moved to Porthcawl on November 23rd, and 300 of them were there organised as two Field Companies, R.E.

Of these 300 however it was found that a considerable number were not so highly skilled as had been originally supposed and those found unsuitable for the Royal Engineers were organised as a separate Company designated the " Unattached Infantry " ; although these men were subsequently returned to the 13th and 15th Battalions of the Welsh Regiment, it is curious to note that a similar organisation obtained for many months in France later on under a slightly different title (" Attached Infantry "). Possibly this close connection with the Royal Engineers in the early days was accountable for the reputation as diggers which the 114th Brigade earned for themselves at a later date.

At Porthcawl these two Companies commenced recruiting on their own and after moving to Abergavenny on January 27th, they were both so much over strength that the 151st Field Company was formed from them on January 29th.

On April 15th both the 123rd and the 151st Field Companies sent drafts of forty men to the 19th Welsh Regiment (Glamorgan Pioneers). The three Field Companies were all brought out to France by the original commanders who organised them, i.e. respectively Major I. W. Lamonby, Major J. R. N. Kirkwood and Capt. F. H. Cory. The Divisional Signal Company was also formed at Porthcawl on the 18th November and moved to Abergavenny with the two Field Companies.

CYCLIST COMPANY.

The Divisional Cyclist Company was formed at Conway on the 22nd of April, 1915, and had their Headquarters in the Town Hall, and was composed of drafts from Infantry Battalions of the Division and also of men recruited direct.

Lieut. R. E. Burrell of the 15th Royal Welsh Fusiliers (London Welsh) was the first C.O. The Company remained at Conway till the move to Winchester.

DIVISIONAL TRAIN.

The Divisional Train was first raised at Cardiff where they remained at Sophia Gardens with the 13th Welsh and "A" Battery, 120th Brigade, R.F.A. (then No. 1 Battery) until the general exodus from that place which happened in November. On the 24th of that month the Train joined the remainder of the Divisional Troops who were forming at Porthcawl and at that time the Train was 250 strong. They remained there until February 2nd, when they moved to Portmadoc. Eight officers and 530 men had now joined and the Train was now organised as four companies and remained at Portmadoc with the 120th Brigade, R.F.A., until the move to Winchester.

Draught horses began to arrive in small numbers about the middle of April and six waggons were issued about the same time.

R.A.M.C.

In November, 1914, the Order of St. John of Jerusalem offered to raise complete unit composed of experienced Ambulance men for the Welsh Army Corps. This offer was accepted by the War Office and what became the 130th (St. John) Field Ambulance was organised at Cardiff early in December.

The whole of the men who formed this unit had had three or four years' training in first-aid, stretcher work, and nursing before enlistment and, being mostly miners, had had frequent opportunity of putting their training into actual practice under most difficult conditions before war began. Most of them belonged to No. 11 District, St. John Ambulance Brigade, and were training in camp when the war broke out.

By Divisional Order No. 11 of the 19th March, 1915, the N.C.O.'s and men of this unit were authorised to wear the St. John's Badge on the left arm.

The unit was designated the 2nd (St. John) Field Ambulance of the 43rd Welsh Division.

In January, 1915, there existed at Porthcawl in addition to the Artillery, R.E., and A.S.C., a body of men (recruits) under training as R.A.M.C. On the 15th of the month the present 129th Field Ambulance was formed from these recruits and designated the " First Field Ambulance, 43rd (Welsh) Division." On the same day the remainder of the available men were formed into the " Third Field Ambulance " (to become later the 131st Field Ambulance). The Second was already in existence at Porthcawl where it had arrived from Cardiff on the 29th December.

On the 29th January the First and Third moved to Criccieth and the second to Portmadoc, but the latter rejoined the fold again at Criccieth on the 17th February and all three ambulances moved to Prestatyn on the 2nd March, where they remained till the move to Winchester.

On the 27th March the numbers of the Ambulances was changed from First, Second and Third, to 129th, 130th (St. John) and 131st.

NOTES.

The Division was faced with the same difficulties which confronted all new Divisions the chief of which was lack of equipment and clothing.

With the exception of the 130th (St. John) Field Ambulance who wore their St. John's Ambulance uniform for the first three months, most of the Division were clothed in Brethyn Llwyd, the Welsh cloth, until supplies of Khaki were received.

Most of the evacuation of sick during the early days was done by the Stafford Howard Ambulance car which had been presented to the Division and did excellent work. The 13th and 16th Royal Welsh Fusiliers both had one company (B " Company in each case) composed at first of men who were especially enlisted with a view to obtaining commissions ; these two companies therefore in reality formed a branch of the O.T.C.

The Division originally comprised four battalions of Bantams of whom no mention has been made above ; they were the 18th and 19th Royal Welsh Fusiliers, the 12th South Wales Borderers and the 17th Welsh.

These Battalions were left behind in North Wales when the Division moved to Winchester and formed part of another Division.

CHAPTER II.

TRAINING AT HOME.

THANKS to the fact that units generally were able to get a fair number of officers and other ranks who had served before to teach the men their duties the Division soon began to present a very favourable appearance. From May, 1915, onwards a series of Brigade field days and staff rides were held.

It was decided to give very little training in trench warfare as it was thought that there would be no difficulty in learning that in France, while the opportunities for training in open warfare would be but few. This proved of the greatest value in giving a bias to moving as opposed to stagnant warfare, and brought success to the Division in sixteen Battles.

While in Wales, the wide distribution of the Division from Rhyl in the north to Abergavenny in the south prevented any training of the Division as a whole. However in August, 1915, the Division was gradually concentrated at Winchester and given full opportunities for training on the very suitable terrain at that place.

In September the Division was inspected by Lt.-Gen. Sir Archibald Murray who reported so favourably that the Division was placed in the fourth 100000, though it really belonged to the fifth 100000, and it was warned to be ready to proceed to France about the end of November.

The paucity of rifles issued to the Division had hitherto rendered musketry instruction, so far as range firing was concerned, a slow process, but rifles were at last issued mostly in the last fortnight at home, and by the most strenuous endeavours, and the using of ranges on Salisbury Plain as well as at Winchester every man was eventually put through a course before embarkation.

November was a busy month, the depot units being separated out, and all units being brought on to the War Establishment.

In the absence of His Majesty the King who was unfortunately unwell, the Division was reviewed on Crawley Down on the 29th November, 1915, by Her Majesty the Queen who was accompanied by H.R.H. Princess Mary. A slight drizzle somewhat marred the day, which was otherwise a great success, Her Majesty being graciously pleased to express her extreme satisfaction with all the arrangements for the review.

During the next few days, with the exception of the Artillery which remained behind to fire a course at Larkhill, the units of the division marched to Southampton, whence they sailed to Havre and were railed to the neighbourhood of Rocquetoire not far from St. Omer.

The move was completed on the 5th December, 1915, and the Division became part of the 11th Corps then under the command of Sir Richard Haking, K.C.B., D.S.O. Towards the end of the December the artillery of the Division arrived and the whole Division moved to St. Venant where it relieved the 46th Division in Corps reserve.

Chapter III.

EARLY DAYS IN FRANCE.

A week after arriving in France about one-third of the Division was attached for a week at a time to the Guards and 19th Division then in the line by Fangissart and Neuve Chapelle respectively

The enemy at that time were fairly quiet, a quietude enforced on both sides by the unusual and extremely wet state of the soil. This enabled the Division to have a favourable opportunity of learning its duties in trench warfare.

In January, 1916, the Division took over the Neuve Chapelle sector of the line from the 19th Division, and from this period till the beginning of June it was continually in the line holding in turn every portion of the 11th Corps' line from Givenchy on the south to Picantin on the north.

During this period there is but little to record except steady progress in obtaining an ascendancy over the enemy and the carrying out of several raids, the most successful of which was that carried out by the 15th Royal Welsh Fusiliers (London Welsh). This was mentioned in General Headquarters' despatches as being the third best raid carried out so far in the British Army. The raiding party while out in No Man's land came across an enemy wiring party just finishing their work. Captain Goronwy Owen, commanding the raid, altered his plans on the spot, and with his raiding party quietly followed the working party into their lines and then set upon them.

The enemy were taken by surprise and the greater portion of them were killed whilst trying to get grenades out of a grenade store.

During this period, Givenchy with its many mines, constant trench mortaring, and numerous springs that involved frequent repairs to trenches was the hardest part of the line to hold.

On June the 10th whilst holding the line near Neuve Chapelle the Division received orders to proceed south to take part in the Somme fighting of 1916. On the 11th the whole Division had handed over to the 61st Division and commenced its move south.

It halted for a fortnight just east of St. Pol where it trained on a manœuvre area lent by the French authorities. A trench to trench attack in all its varieties was practised. The Division then moved further south and at Rubempre joined the 2nd Corps, then commanded by Sir Claude Jacob, K.C.B., D.S.O.

At this time the verbal orders received were that the Division as part of the 2nd Corps was to be prepared to follow the Cavalry in the event of a break through and take over Bapaume from them.

The check received by the centre and left of the British attack on the 1st July altered these plans and after marching first north towards Acheux and then south to Treux the Division eventually joined the 15th Corps under Sir Henry Horne, K.C.B., and on the 5th July relieved the 7th Division in the village of Mametz, and was ordered to prepare for the capture of Mametz Wood.

CHAPTER IV.

CAPTURE OF MAMETZ WOOD.

THE task that lay before the Division was one of some magnitude. So difficult had it been thought that in the orders for the attack on the 1st July General Headquarters had left out Mametz wood in their orders, though British troops were to have moved forward to the east and west of it. Moreover, it was capable of being reinforced easily, the German second line system being only 300 yards from its northern edge. The 6th to the 9th July were spent in reconnaissance and in testing the enemy's strength by small attacks.

On the 7th July the 115th Brigade made a small attack on the eastern edge of the wood. Two separate attacks were made that day at 8 a.m. and 11 a.m. by the 16th (Cardiff City) Welsh and the 10th South Wales Borderers (1st Gwents), but neither were successful owing to machine-gun fire not only from the wood but also from some small copses to the north named Hatiron and Sabot respectively. The fire from these enfiladed the attack which in both cases just failed to reach the wood.

On the 9th July it was decided that the time was ripe to attack the wood with the full weight of the Division, and this was carried out at 4.15 a.m. on the 10th July. The task of capturing the eastern portion of the wood was allotted to the 114th Brigade and the western portion to the 113th Brigade, the 115th Brigade being kept in reserve near Minden post and Mametz.

c

At 3.30 a.m. on the 10th July a heavy concentrated fire was directed on the southern edge of the wood and a smoke barrage was put up on the eastern and south-western portions of the wood. The last was successful in drawing the fire of the enemy while our troops attacked between. At 4.15 a.m. the Infantry advanced with the 13th Welsh (2nd Rhonddas) on the right, the 14th Welsh (Swansea) in the centre and the 16th Royal Welsh Fusiliers on the left. This was one of the most magnificent sights of the war. In the words of officers of a neighbouring division wave after wave of men were seen advancing without hesitation and without a break over a distance which in some places was nearly 500 yards. The 14th Welsh speedily cleared their portion of the wood, Captain Wilson distinguishing himself by bayonetting in solitary combat at the head cf his Company a burly German, and then bringing down with a shot a sniper in a tree. Lieut. Hawkins did equally good if not better work by charging down on two separate machine guns, both of which he captured though unfortunately he was wounded the second time.

The 13th Welsh on the right encountered severe re-sistance and had eventually to be reinforced by the 15th (Caermarthen) Welsh. A party of the latter broke through the Germans, but eventually had to cut their way back, one company under Captain Lewis returning with only seven survivors. Eventually the 13th, 14th and 15th Welsh formed a line just south of the most southern cross ride eastwards from its junction with the main ride.

On the left the 16th Royal Welsh Fusiliers, who had not kept quite close enough to our artillery barrage, were met by heavy rifle and machine-gun fire and twice repulsed, their gallant Colonel Ronald Carden being killed, but re-inforced by the 15th Royal Welsh Fusiliers both Battalions entered the wood and arrived at the southern ride. Wood support trench was however still held by the Germans and from here an enfilading machine gun prevented their further advance through the wood, and the gap between these Battalions and the 14th Welsh was filled by the 10th Welsh under Lt.-Col. Ricketts, who was unfortunately wounded. The Engineers and Pioneers (19th Welsh) were ordered up and a trench was dug along the southern ride and wired. By 1 p.m. wood support trench was cleared by the 13th Royal Welsh Fusiliers under Lt.-Col. O Flower, who later on was unfortunately killed by a shell.

The troops were now reorganised, and the 10th South Wales Borderers and 17th Royal Welsh Fusiliers were sent up to reinforce the 114th Brigade.

At 4 p.m. a further advance was made which brought the troops to the northern end of the wood. The 10th South Wales Borderers captured the eastern portion of the wood in gallant style, the Germans who fled towards Sabot copse suffering heavily from our machine guns in Caterpillar and Marlborough woods. The 15th Welsh east of the central ride, and the 17th and 15th Royal Welsh Fusiliers west of it fought their way up to 40 yards from the north edge of the wood where they were held up by heavy rifle and machine-gun fire from the German second line. Preparations were then made to hold for the night a line some distance behind the edge of the wood. During the night the remainder of the 115th Infantry Brigade, the 11th South Wales Borderers and 16th Welsh were brought up and the 113th and 114th Infantry Brigades were withdrawn.

On the 11th July at 3.15 p.m. the 115th Brigade advanced and cleared out the Germans on the northern edge of the wood. That same evening the 21st Division relieved the Division in Mametz wood and the 38th moved eventually to Coigneux, where it relieved the 48th Division taking over the line just south of Hebuterne and Gommecourt and opposite Serre.

The Division now belonged to the 8th Corps under Sir Aylmer Hunter Weston and moved with that Corps to Ypres about the end of August. Thus closed the Division's share in the Somme fighting, in which in two days it took the largest wood captured in the same, and took some 400 odd prisoners from five different regiments.

CHAPTER V.

YPRES.

AFTER a short period in reserve at Esquelbesques the Division took over the line just north of Ypres opposite the Pilckem Ridge. This part of the line it held till June, 1917, except for one short break at Christmas, 1916, when it was in reserve.

By the careful grading of trenches the Division soon turned a mass of muddy trenches into dry, comfortable ones which earned the special commendation of Lord Cavan when the Division became part of the 14th Corps. The Division spent a comparatively quiet time here, punctuated only by raids which were gradually carried out more frequently and on a larger scale as time went on. One of the most successful was carried out by the 114th Brigade who brought some twenty prisoners out of the famous High Command Redoubt and killed some fifty Germans with the bayonet.

CHAPTER VI.

ATTACK ON THE PILCKEM RIDGE.

TOWARDS the end of May, 1917, when the Division was holding the British line from the Ypres-Pilckem road to Boesinghe inclusive, it was informed that a big attack would be delivered by the British on the Ypres front and that advantage should be taken of the coming attack of the Second Army on the Messines-Wytschaete Ridge to dig such assembly trenches as would be necessary. These trenches were dug towards the end of May and the beginning of June, and our line advanced all along this front to within 200 yards of the enemy front line, from, in some places, a distance of 300 yards further off.

The enemy's attention was drawn to these trenches but he did comparatively little firing upon them, and it was thought that he must have considered them as a ruse to try and draw attention from the attack upon the Messines-Wytschaete Ridge.

In June the Division was informed of the definite role that it would have to play in the coming Battle.

It then left the 8th Corps and joined the 14th Corps and in course of time handed over the Boesinghe sector to the Guards Division, who were to fight on their left.

Towards the end of June the Division left the line and proceeded to the St. Hilaire area to train for the coming Battle.

A replica of the trenches and strong points to be attacked was laid out on the ground between Enquin and Liettres and the Brigades were practiced over the same in their respective roles. Opportunity was also taken to practice the machine-gun barrage and this was found extremely useful, as none of the machine gunners had hitherto done any firing for long periods.

On the 19th and 20th July the Division returned to its sector in the line, taking over from the 29th Division, who had carried on such work as was necessary in preparation for the attack.

From the period the Division was in the line until the day of the actual attack on the 31st July a considerable number of losses were occurred from shell fire and gas shells. The Germans had introduced new gas of the mustard type which proved much more serious than at first sight it appeared to be. Matters, however, proceeded well and all arrangements were completed some days before the attack actually took place.

On the morning of the 27th July aeroplane reports indicated that the Germans had evacuated their trenches and it was arranged that the Division and the Guards should send forward patrols at 5.30 in the afternoon to test the accuracy of the above report.

The 15th Welsh Regiment and the 15th Royal Welsh Fusiliers were detailed to each find two Platoons for this work.

At the appointed hour they moved forward and found no Germans in the front line but after proceeding beyond this discovered that the support and reserve lines and also the German second line system were strongly held. The platoons however, pushed on until they had fully developed the enemy's strength, which on the western slope of the Pilckem Ridge was found to be two battalions.

In the front of the Guards owing to the severity of the shelling the enemy had withdrawn from his front system and arrangements were consequently made by which the left of the Division was linked up with the right of what the Guards had gained east of the Yser Canal, so as to facilitate their further attack.

On the night 30th/31st July the troops were brought into their assembly positions and were concentrated without a hitch by 2.54 a.m. on the 31st July.

The general dispositions of the Division were as under :—

114th Brigade on the right and the
113th Brigade on the left with the
115th Brigade in reserve.

Tasks allotted to the first two Brigades were to capture the village of Pilckem and the Pilckem Ridge up to half-way between the River Steenbeek and Pilckem Village. On this line being attained the 115th Infantry Brigade were to push through two Battalions to capture the Steenbeek and its crossings.

The troops suffered but little loss before the attack commenced and this is attributed to the plentiful bombardment by gas shell of enemy batteries.

Zero was at 3.50 a.m. and at that hour the 10th Welsh Regiment on the right, and the 13th Welsh Regiment on the right centre, the 13th Royal Welsh Fusiliers on the left centre and the 16th Royal Welsh Fusiliers on the left moved forward to the attack.

The Blue Line was captured with but little opposition, most of the enemy encountered being found in dugouts in Caesar's Support. These were taken prisoners, with the exception of those who showed fight.

The advance to the Black Line, just east of Pilckem, was carried out by the 15th Welsh Regiment on the right centre and the 14th Welsh Regiment on the right.

In the 113th Brigade who had not so many trenches to encounter this attack was carried out by the remaining two Companies in both the 13th Royal Welsh Fusiliers and 16th Royal Welsh Fusiliers. Opposition made in this advance was severer than that made in the advance on the Blue Line. The centres of resistance were Harsouin Farm and Stray Farm on the right and the village of Pilckem on the left. In all these places there were several concrete machine-gun implacements but the men working very well outflanked them and compelled the garrisons to surrender.

The Black Line was captured up to time and was immediately consolidated.

The advance to the Green Line was carried out by half Battalions of the 15th and 14th Welsh Regiment on the right and by the 15th Royal Welsh Fusiliers on the left.

Considerable trouble was met from the direction of Rudolphe Farm which was in the area allotted to the 51st Division. That Division was either not up or was too much to the right and consequently a Platoon of the 15th Welsh Regiment was detailed to attack the farm. This was successfully accomplished. The enemy, with the exception of some fifteen men who surrendered, either ran away or were shot.

The neighbourhood of Iron Cross was strongly held and the 14th Welsh Regiment suffered somewhat heavily in rushing it. They had, however, the satisfaction of killing with the bayonet some twenty of the enemy and taking forty prisoners and three machine guns in this neighbourhood. This done the 14th Welsh Regiment pushed on to U. 28   10.35 where an enemy dressing station and sixteen wounded and twenty-two men were captured.

The 15th Royal Welsh Fusiliers commenced their advance from the Blue Line at the correct time but on nearing Battery Copse were met there with such heavy fire that in a short time only a few officers were left and our barrage began to run away from the men. The men, however, struggled forward and established themselves on the Iron Cross Ridge.

During the period that 113th and 114th Brigades were attacking up to the Iron Cross Ridge the 11th South Wales Borderers and the 17th Royal Welsh Fusiliers, both of the 115th Brigade were gradually working their way forward until they were close up to the Iron Cross Ridge from which they launched their attack, on the Steenbeek. This attack was successfully carried out in the face of considerable opposition from concrete shelters inside the houses, most of which were made by machine guns. All were, however, outflanked by the Infantry and the garrisons compelled to surrender and the Steenbeek was reached and parties pushed across to cover and hold its crossings.

The losses amongst our men were however severe and consequently the General Officer commanding the 115th Infantry Brigade ordered one Company of the 16th Welsh Regiment to reinforce the 17th Royal Welsh Fusiliers and one Company of the 10th South Wales Borderers to reinforce the 11th South Wales Borderers. From 2 p.m. onwards, Germans were seen to be massing for counter-attack and this attack developed at 3.10 p.m. and one Company of the 11th South Wales Borderers which had occupied Au Bon Gite were forced to retire to the western side of the Steenbeek. The remainder of the line held repelled the attack, the artillery and machine-gun b rrage helping largely. Rifle fire was successfully employed in wiping out some 100 Germans who had got through our barrage.

During the course of the afternoon the weather which had been dull and cloudy changed for the worse and rain began to fall steadily and continued more or less for the next three days, rendering operations extremely difficult owing to the slippery and muddy nature of the ground, which clogged the movement of the Infantry.

The morning of the 31st of August was quiet so far as hostilities were concerned but in course of the afternoon the enemy again attempted a counter-attack, but this was broken up by artillery and machine-gun fire before it had time to mature.

The heavy shelling and the state of the weather and the many casualties experienced by the 115th Brigade necessitated its being relieved.

On the night of the 1st/2nd August the 113th Brigade took over the front line. From this date up to the 6th August there is but little to record whatever, the weather during this period being so bad that operations became impossible. On the 6th the Division was relieved in the line by the 20th Division and withdrew to Proven where it rested and recommenced training.

The Division remained at Proven until the 19th and 20th August, when it relieved the 20th Division, who in the meanwhile had taken Langemarck.

The line taken over ran through White Trench and Bear Trench, Eagle Trench being in the hands of the Germans.

In conjunction with larger attacks on the right an attack was made at 1.55 p.m. on the 27th August by the 16th Welsh Regiment.

The weather which had been moderately fine in the morning became so bad during the course of the day that when the time came to advance, the men who had been lying in shell-holes which were gradually filling with water found great difficulty in getting out and advancing and keeping up with the barrage. The barrage got away from them and they came under the fire of machine guns from the direction of Pheasant Farm and were unable to reach their objective.

No further operations were conducted on the front of the Division and the remaining period in the line passed without event except for the usual daily shelling.

The Division was relieved on the 11th September by the 20th Division and moved to Proven and left Proven on the 13th September for Croix du Bac, where it took over from the 57th Division the British line near Armentieres.

The success in taking Pilckem Ridge may be attributed to the excellent work done by the artillery in breaking down the wire and smashing up trenches and emplacements and also to the way in which the men rapidly outflanked numerous concrete dugouts met in the area captured. The first enumeration stated that there were 280 of these.

Opposed to the Division on the morning of the 31st July was the German 3rd Guards Division, just arrived in the line the day before in place of the 23rd Reserve Division, worn out by our preparatory activity.

Of the 3rd Guards Division, the Guards Fusilier Regiment (the notorious " Cockchafers " so popular in Berlin) which was holding Pilckem itself received particularly rough treatment at the hands of the Division. All three Battalions were met and broken in turn and of this regiment alone 400 prisoners were taken as well as many killed.

Of the other regiments of the 3rd Guards Division the Lehr Regiment was surprised while still relieving the 392nd I.R., 3rd Reserve Division, and prisoners of both regiments were taken, while a few prisoners were taken of the 9th Grenadiers who were in reserve and who suffered heavy losses in counter-attacking the Steenbeek. In addition a number of prisoners were taken of the 73rd Fusiliers (Hanoverians), 111th Division, who just overlapped into our left front, making a total of close on 700 prisoners. The 3rd Guards Division had to be withdrawn immediately after the Battle.

In the course of the subsequent operations between the 20th August and 11th September prisoners were taken from the 119th Grenadier and 125th Infantry Regiments of the 26th (Wurtenberg) Division and from the 185th Infantry Regiment of the 208th Division which relieved the 26th Division, withdrawn exhausted, from the effects of our shell fire.

CHAPTER VII.

TRENCH WARFARE NEAR ARMENTIERES.

From September, 1917, *to March,* 1918.

FROM the middle of September, 1917, to the end of March, 1918, the Division was engaged in trench warfare pure and simple.

During this period the front held by the Division was not at all times the same and several exchanges of front took place with Divisions on the flanks, but the various parts of the line held extended from Laventie to Armentieres and at times the Division was holding as much as ten miles of front ; at these times, of course, all three Brigades were in the line and reliefs were few and far between.

The country is much the same as Flanders and this period of trench warfare was almost as much a war against water and natural conditions as against the enemy ; all arms were busy at all times in improving and maintaining the enormous system of trenches, and the Royal Engineers and Pioneers could only be employed in the more skilled work and on drainage. This latter work was at times almost a matter of life and death, all trenches had to be considered as drains and had to be carefully graduated as such and in an absolutely flat country this was extremely difficult ; but certain it was that if a trench was not cleared out and repaired at once after it had been blown in by a shell, not only that trench but all its neighbours were immediately flooded.

After a spell of bad weather this flooding of the trenches occurred without the assistance of the enemy while some trenches, despite all efforts, were never anything better than very wet drains in which one could move unseen by the enemy.

This flat country however had its compensations. The enemy certainly held the Aubers Ridge which overlooked our lines, but this ridge was some way back from his front line and the country was fairly well covered with scattered trees and overgrown hedges ; consequently, it was possible in places to approach quite close to our front line without being seen and the various isolated cottages near the line escaped bombardment ; these cottages were chiefly used as battalion headquarters and several of them were christened with familiar sounding names such as " Killay Hall," " Eaton Hall," " Arden," etc. Those actually in the trench system were not so comfortable and as this part of the line had not moved since the end of 1914, there was not much masonry left ; one of these farms, called " Burnt Farm," was said to be the original of Bairnsfather's sketch " We are billeted in a farm."

A ruined monastery actually in the front line was it is believed, the birthplace of the Green Chartreuse liqueur.

During this period Major-Generals Trial and Allen of the U.S. Army were attached to Divisional Headquarters for a fortnight in each case ; they were each accompanied by a Chief of Staff and one other Staff Officer.

The Portuguese Corps was at this time holding the line near Laventie and previous to their taking over that line all the battalions of the 1st Portuguese Division were attached to the Welsh Division for instruction in the trenches. The Australian Corps were on our left north of the River Lys.

Towards the end of the year 1917 it became evident to the Higher Command that the enemy contemplated a decisive offensive on the western front and that on this front the Allies could not hope to take the offensive at any rate during the early part of the next year. Orders were therefore received that all parts of the British line were to be strengthened by every conceivable means. From then onwards therefore until the end of March the Division was heavily at work in constructing rear lines of defence as far back as the northern bank of the Lys and an almost inconceivable amount of concrete and barbed wire was erected in the sector ; all battalions who were in reserve were employed daily on new work while those in the line improved the old and everything was done to make this part of the line impregnable.

In the middle of January a most unusual thing happened ; the whole Division came out of the line for rest and training and moved to the area west of Estaires. This is pronounced as unusual because up till now the Division had only been out of the line for a total of two months since it landed in France.

This period of training was rather spoilt by the weather which was so bad that for days at a time some of the farms in which the troops were billeted were completely surrounded by water and could only be approached by wading up to the knees. The training and rest were also further interfered with by the necessity of employing part of the Division on the construction of defences ; indeed, the only training of value was that obtained by moving one brigade at a time to the St. Hilaire area, and two batteries at a time to Westrehem where there was an artillery range.

This was a sad time for the Division in one respect. Orders were received for all brigades in the British Army to be reduced to a strength of three battalions ; four of the battalions in the Division were to be disbanded and the Divisional Commander was not given a free hand in the selection of those battalions.

The 15th Royal Welsh Fusiliers (The London Welsh), The 11th (2nd Gwent Battalion) South Wales Borderers,

The 10th (1st Rhondda Battalion) Welsh Regiment, and the 16th (Cardiff City) Welsh Regiment were consequently disbanded. However, the officers and men of these battalions were not all lost to the Division for permission was given to bring all other battalions up to full strength and many good men and true joined those battalions from the disbanded battalions. Indeed, this reduction in strength, if it was to come at all, could not have come at a more opportune time, for the machine-gun companies were at this time about to be organised as a Battalion, and several members of the new battalion headquarters were selected from the disbanded Infantry Battalions.

The 2nd Royal Welsh Fusiliers joined the 115th Brigade from the 33rd Division on the 6th February and the Division went forward into the line again in the middle of February, reorganised in brigades of three battalions each, but the organisation of the Machine-Gun Companies as a Battalion was not completed until the middle of March.

During the above period of trench warfare many raids were carried out against the enemy, the most notable of which were as follows.

On the night 7th/8th ten officers and 300 men of the 10th South Wales Borderers, under Capt. W. T. Cobb, M.C., raided the German trenches opposite Armentieres on a front of 300 yards and penetrated to a depth of 200 yards. They killed or wounded about fifty-five of the enemy, blew up three concrete dug-outs and brought back fifteen prisoners.

A raid of much the same strength and success was carried out on the 15th March by the 16th Royal Welsh Fusiliers.

During this period the enemy made repeated attempts to raid our trenches and indeed succeeded in entering them on several occasions ; this was easy considering the length of line held and the consequent wide dispersion of our forward posts ; but he never succeeded in capturing any of our men until towards the very end when two men were reported missing. It can be said that our patrols had control of No Man's Land and this was accountable for much of the success of our raids, for it was thus possible to have a thorough previous reconnaissance made of the approaches and the enemy's wire in every case.

The Sniping Company can also be said to have had the upperhand of the enemy's snipers throughout the whole period ; their work could be judged by results and the results were that it was possible to move about unmolested in exposed trenches or even in the open within three or four hundred yards of the enemy's line.

CHAPTER VIII.

ACTION OF THE DIVISIONAL ARTILLERY AT THE BATTLE OF THE LYS.

April and May, 1918

AT the beginning of April 38th Divisional Artillery was in line on the Armentieres front, covering the 34th Division Infantry.

On night 7/8th Armentieres was very heavily bombarded with gas shells : estimated that 40,000 rounds were fired.

122nd Brigade which was in Armentieres itself suffered heavily particularly at Brigade Headquarters, where the Brigade Commander and all other officers, except one, became casualties.

Major W. A. C. Stone took over command of 122nd Brigade on evening of the 8th.

At 4.15 a.m. on 9th the enemy opened a very heavy bombardment on the whole front. Fire was particularly heavy on battery areas. 121st Brigade Headquarters, at La Rolanderie, was shelled and hit, the Orderly Officer was killed and the M.O. wounded. Two 4·5″ Howitzers, " D " 121st Brigade, in a forward position at La Vessee were destroyed.

The enemy attack was launched at about 8 a.m.

The right flank of the attack was well south of Armentieres at about the junction of 34th and 40th (on our right) Divisional fronts : that is to say 34th Division was not attacked.

The situation remained obscure for some time, but at about 10 a.m. information was received that the enemy had broken through the Portuguese front (on right of 40th Division) and that 40th Division was withdrawing.

Before mid-day the enemy were within 500 yards of 121st Brigade Headquarters, 121st Brigade Headquarters, and batteries withdrew under heavy machine-gun fire to previously prepared positions north of River Lys, which was crossed at Armentieres. 122nd Brigade remained in a position in and near the town.

By the evening the enemy had crossed the Lys at Bac St. Maur and was working along the north bank towards Erquinghem. His infantry had also reached Croix du bac, 12 miles from 34th Divisional Headquarters.

The 34th Division had thrown out a defensive right flank and by dark were holding 17,000 yards of front covered by eight batteries, some of which, after having been shooting north-east in the morning were now shooting south-west.

At 5 a.m. on the 10th Divisional Headquarters moved from Steenwerck to Oultersteene.

A fresh attack developed north of Armentieres and made progress. The attack north of the Lys west of Armentieres was continued.

The 121st Brigade which had been in action just north of Erquinghem withdrew to east of Steenwerck. Here about 2 p.m. the Infantry retired through the guns and shortly afterwards the batteries withdrew singly under heavy machine-gun and rifle fire to positions near Steenwerck Station.

The Infantry formed a line in front of the railway embankment behind the guns which were then withdrawn under cover behind the embankment.

About 4.30 p.m. an infantry brigade of the 29th Division de-bussed on the Bailleul-Nieppe Road, passed through the guns and formed a new line along the embankment. Batteries were then withdrawn singly to the Bailleul-Nieppe Road.

These three moves of the batteries were all carried out under machine gun and rifle fire at close range, the total distance retired was well under two miles, and at times the guns actually held the front line and formed rallying points for the infantry.

During these withdrawals the enemy's infantry were at times so close that on one occasion a battery retired under cover of the fire of one of its own Lewis gun, which was mounted on and fired from one of the limbers while on the move.

Meanwhile the 122nd Brigade had withdrawn from Armentieres, first to positions near Pont de Nieppe and later to behind Nieppe.

Armentieres now formed a very pronounced salient and was evacuated on night 10/11th. An anti-tank gun (121st Brigade) which had been in action near Chapelle d'Armentieres was successfullly brought away lashed to the back of an Infantry cooker. The only guns lost were the two Howitzers at La Vesee, destroyed during the preliminary bombardment.

From now onwards the fighting was in the nature of a slow rearguard action—the general trend of the retirement being north-west, through Bailleul to St. Jan Cappel, which was reached on night 15th/16th.

Throughout the withdrawal batteries were always moved back either singly or in pairs in each brigade, all ammunition dumped with the guns being fired before the battery withdrew.

The average rate of harassing fire was sixty rounds per battery per hour, exclusive of bombardments, S.O.S., etc., this rate was found practicable but the strain on the personnel of firing at least 1440 rounds per battery per day was considerable.

The line held fast in front of St. Jan Cappel. Two Brigades of 36th Divisional Artillery came under orders of 38th Divisional Artillery and French reinforcements began to arrive.

The 38th Divisional Artillery was under a French Division from 20th to 24th, when it was withdrawn from the line into Army Reserve (night 24/25th) and marched early 25th to the old waggon lines at Hamhoek.

Kemmel fell on the 25th April and, just as batteries were unharnessing, orders were received that 38th Divisional Artillery was to be attached to 25th Division. The latter in conjunction with the French were to counter-attack at 3 a.m. on 26th.

Batteries moved into action after dark along the Scherpenberg Beek. Owing to the depth of the final objective (4000 yards) these positions had to be close up : some of them were not more than 1500 yards from the front line.

Barrage orders reached Brigades only about an hour before zero, but all batteries were ready in time and fired the barrage.

The 25th Division attack was successful and reached Kemmel village. Owing, however, to the French on the right being held up 25th Divisional troops had to be withdrawn in daylight on 26th to their original line and, in consequence, batteries were in very exposed positions and were withdrawn on night 26/27th to positions on the Groot Beek north-east of Reninghelst.

On 29th the enemy made a determined effort to capture the Mont Noir-Scherpenberg Ridge and batteries were firing S.O.S. and counter-preparation for hours on end. The attack, which was the last made by the enemy in this region, failed completely.

The following letters were received after the Battle :—

25TH DIVISION, No. G385.

G. O. C., R.A.,
    38th Div. Artillery.

      " Will you please accept my best thanks for the assistance you have given the 25th Division since April 26th. Will you also, in the name of the 25th Division, thank your officers and men for the really excellent work they have done.

During the period you and your people have been with us a considerable amount of praise has been given to the Division. Some of this is no doubt due to the Infantry but the Artillery, which takes its share, and a very large one, in any operation, successful or otherwise, must also take a full share of the credit or criticism which results.

During the hours which culminated in the counter-attack on Kemmel Village on the morning of the 26th the Artillery had a more difficult task than the Infantry, as it had little daylight to get into action or get up the necessary ammunition to prepare to carry out an extensive barrage programme at 3 a.m. The result was very successful as far as the combined action of the units which composed the Division on that date were concerned.

On the 29th when the Germans undoubtedly launched a serious attack the Infantry ' stuck it ' really well, but the main reason of the attack being beaten off was the rapidity and accuracy with which the gunners answered the S.O.S. call. Since then the Infantry have had a comparatively easy time, but the Artillery have been working at full pressure day and night. The Infantry assure me they have as much confidence in 38th Divisional Artillery as in 25th Divisional Artillery, and all ranks send you their hearty thanks."

(Sd.) E. T. G. BAINBRIDGE,
Major General,
3rd May, 1918.　　　　　Commanding 25th Division.

38th Divisional Artillery.

" This Artillery was covering the front held by the Division on the 9th April and continued to do so throughout the operations.

During the whole period from the 9th April when it

covered a front of approximately 18.000 yards, to the time when the Infantry of the Division was withdrawn from the line on the 21st April, this Artillery fought magnificently and by its steady accurate fire gave ever increasing confidence to the Infantry, enabling it to beat off many hostile attacks.

The successive retirements which had to be made were most skilfully and rapidly carried out in such a manner that at no time was the retiring Infantry without the covering fire of at least one Group. No guns were lost except two Field Howitzers in a forward position at La Vesse, which were destroyed by hostile fire on the 9th April.

The record of these days is one of which the 38th Divisional Artillery may well be proud."

(Sd.) L. NICHOLSON,

Major General.

23/4/1918. Commanding 34th Division.

CHAPTER IX.

THE MOVE SOUTH TO OPPOSE THE GERMAN OFFENSIVE.

Stationary Warfare near Albert.

April till July, 1918.

THE enemy had commenced the great offensive opposite Amiens on March 21st, and the Division was moved south with considerable speed at the end of the month to help to oppose this offensive. To the great regret of the rest of the Division the Artillery were left behind to support the 34th Division which relieved us in the line. No one could forecast at this time that the Artillery were so soon to be in the thick of the fight and were to play such a large part in withstanding the German attempts to reach Calais.

On the 29th March the whole of the Division were in the line near Armentieres with the exception of the 113th Brigade who were in close support at Erquinghem, but by the 2nd April the whole Division (except the Artillery) was concentrated five miles north-west of Albert (with one brigade in rear at Talmas) prepared to relieve the 47th and 2nd Divisions the next day.

These two divisions had been badly knocked about during the German advance of the previous ten days and were holding a line west of the Ancre from Albert to Hamel ; here they had succeeded in temporarily arresting the enemy's onrush, but he had troops west of the Ancre and was holding Albert and the high ground between Albert and Bouzincourt in some strength, and it was consequently possible for him to pass troops through Albert and mass them for attack west of the river. Consequently although the intended relief was postponed and the Division was retained in Army Reserve yet all units had to be in continual readiness to move and the Division had to be prepared for all eventualities.

On the 3rd April the 113th Brigade was withdrawn to Toutencourt.

On the completion of that move the Division was disposed as follows :—115th Brigade, 151st Field Company, R.E., and " C " Machine Gun Company at Hedauville in close support of the Divisions in the line, prepared to reinforce any part of the line but also working all day on the preparation of defences ; the remainder of the Division about Toutencourt and Talmas with their attention directed towards the south where the enemy were advancing at Villers Bretonneux and Montdidier. They also renewed their attack against the Australians on the Somme and at midnight on the 4/5th orders were received for the Division to be prepared to move at one hour's notice.

The following day the 113th Brigade moved to a position of readiness near Contay and bivouacked in the open for the night ; the 114th Brigade moved forward to Herissartt and were accommodated partly in billets and partly in tents.

The hostile attacks were however held up and on the evening of the 6th the 114th Brigade returned whence they came but 113th Brigade moved into billets at Rubempre.

Another series of moves occurred on the 10th ; indeed, such was the unavoidable number of moves at this period and the congestion of troops in this area, that it was a relief when the order was received to relieve the 12th Division in the line opposite Albert on the night of the 11/12th.

The line that the Division took over consisted of hastily made and only partially finished trenches and of old trenches dating back to 1914 and, where the line ran between Bouzincourt and Aveluy, the enemy held the high ground and it was here impossible to see into the Ancre Valley.

Consequently, orders were received that the Division was to capture this ground while the 35th Division on our left improved their position in Aveluy Wood and the Australians on our right lent the assistance of their Artillery. The attack took place at 7.30 p.m. on the 22nd April and was entrusted to the 113th Brigade and 2nd Royal Welsh Fusiliers. Although owing to the strength of the enemy's position and his numerous machine guns and artillery the attack did not succeed in driving the enemy completely off the plateau, yet it succeeded in advancing our line a distance of 250 yards on a frontage of 1000 yards and denied the enemy the observation of our positions, which he had previously enjoyed, and gained a position where the Ancre Valley could be seen. Two officers and eighty-three other ranks were taken prisoners and six machine guns were captured ; the attack therefore can be described as a decided success, but it was a costly operation and some of the attacking companies were reduced to a strength of thirty men.

The 13th Royal Welsh Fusiliers who were on the right were most successful and also sustained the greatest number of casualties, eight officers and 263 other ranks ; " D " Company, under Capt. C. B. Williams, M.C., it was who reached and held on to their final objective which gave us the above mentioned observation into the Ancre Valley ; this company were heavily counter-attacked the next morning at 4.40 a.m. and again at 7.30 p.m. but held their ground. During the night the Field Ambulances evacuated 400 wounded between 7.30 p.m. and 7 a.m. The regimental bearers were assisted by the Pioneers after

the latter had completed their work of consolidation and
Private G. Stewkesbury of that Battalion was awarded
the D.C.M. for his gallantry in connection with this ;
though wounded in the right eye and nearly blind he continued stretcher bearing until he fainted after being
wounded a second time. The Brigade remained on the
position that it had won until the night of the 25th when
it was relieved by the 115th Brigade and withdrew into
reserve close at hand.

On the 27th part of the line was taken over by the
Australians leaving the 115th Brigade in occupation of the
battle ground won by the 113th Brigade ; 115th Brigade
continued to hold this part of the line until the 20th May,
and during that period improved their position there by
an operation carried out by the 17th Royal Welsh Fusiliers
on the 1st May.

On the 9th May the enemy made a determined attack
in force against this high ground which he had always dis-
puted strongly and which he evidently considered most
important ; at the same time he attacked the Australians
on our right, both attacks being preceded by an excep-
tionally heavy bombardment.

He succeeded in driving the Australians back from their
front line but the right of the 115th Brigade held by " C "
and " D " Companies, 17th Royal Welsh Fusiliers, held
on all day with their flank exposed until a counter-attack
by the Australians restored the situation the next night.

During this attack the enemy tried the old trick of
shouting " Retire " as they advanced, but found that
there was " nothing doing " as regards the Welsh Division.

Meanwhile, the 113th and 114th Brigades had three
days' rest in the neighbourhood of Toutencourt and than
moved forward again on the 1st and 2nd May, to relieve
the 35th Division in Aveluy Wood ; the Division thus
held the line from opposite Aveluy to Mesnil with all their
brigades in the line.

The position of this line in Aveluy Wood and immediately south of it was far from satisfactory, the enemy being in possession of the crest of the ridge which runs parallel to the river.

It was therefore decided to attack him along this line on the 10th May ; this had been done by the 35th Division without success, for Aveluy Wood was composed of saplings and bushes which were in places practically impenetrable ; it was therefore very difficult for troops to maintain any cohesion in attack, the natural dash of the attacking troops was at a discount, and it was impossible to bombard the wood heavily beforehand for fear of turning these young trees into a veritable abattis of broken branches.

The 35th Division had attacked from the west and in order to vary the programme and create an element of surprise it was decided that our attack should be made from the north ; this meant that the attacking troops must advance with their line at right angles to the enemy's front, an operation which would have been impossible on open ground and which entailed considerable difficulties in forming up for attack, for the left of the attacking lines had to form up not more than 20 yards from the enemy's front posts and then advance across the front of those posts. All these difficulties were, however, overcome by the 114th Brigade and the assembly and commencement of the attack was carried out according to plan.

The attack was made by the 15th Welsh and two companies of the 14th Welsh.

After the attack had commenced, part of the artillery barrage suddenly fell short owing to an accident and continued to do so, playing havoc with the front line and supports : such was the loss and disorganisation caused by this that the attack had to be abandoned.

On the 20th May the Division came out of the line for a fortnight's rest after a successful raid had been carried out by the 14th and 16th Royal Welsh Fusiliers on the 18th. The enemy at this time made several attempts to rush our posts in Aveluy Wood but without success. The Division was at Toutencourt, Herissart, and Rubompre until June 3rd, when we relieved the 63rd Division.

On the day on which the Division came out of the line it was found necessary that Major-General Blackader should undergo a course of treatment at the Pasteur Institute in Paris. It was not known when he left that this course would be of a lengthy duration and would necessitate his relinquishing command of the Division.

The Division had therefore no opportunity of bidding him farewell or of expressing their unbounded regret at the departure of their General, who had commanded the Division with such success for two years and who had during that time become beloved and respected by all.

During this period of " rest " two battalions were always employed on the improvement of defences and the Machine Gun Battalion was frequently engaged in support of minor operations of the divisions in the line. The remainder of the Division was hard at work training, for considerable drafts had been and were now being received ; the chief part of the training consisted in musketry and a rifle meeting was held on the day before the Division went into the line again. The results of this musketry training were obvious during the fighting which commenced in August.

On the 23rd May Major-General T. A. Cubitt, C.M.G., D.S.O., arrived to take command of the Division.

There was at this time a great shortage of men throughout the whole Army and strenuous efforts had to be made to avoid decreasing the strength of battalions. For this reason the Divisional Sniping Company was disbanded and rejoined their battalions on the 1st June.

This Company had been in existence since August 10th, 1916, and had certainly earned its place in the team ; it was organised in sections, the men of each section all belonging to the same Brigade, and there was a healthy rivalry between the sections ; so much so, that the only occasion when there was any unpleasantness between them arose when one section was relieved by another in Aveluy Wood ; the former wished to refuse to be relieved on the score that Aveluy Wood was the best (Bosche) hunting ground ever discovered and that they had found it first.

The Division remained in the line from Aveluy Wood inclusive to Hamel until July 19th. During this time our patrols had complete control of " No Man's Land," but although encounters in the wood were frequent and the enemy here often tried to rush our posts yet in the open to the north he was extremely hard to locate, sometimes occupying one series of posts, sometimes another, and our patrols would be out for hours at a time with the object of locating the enemy and capturing a post.

At last it was apparent that he intended to occupy the site of Hamel Village permanently and the 2nd Royal Welsh Fusiliers brought off a successful raid against that place on the 11th July, and after some stiff fighting brought back nineteen prisoners and a machine gun.

During one of the enemy's attempts to rush our posts in Aveluy Wood, Private L. Stephens, " D " Company, 2nd Royal Welsh Fusiliers, won the D.C.M. by defending his post single handed although wounded, the remainder of the men of the post having been either killed or wounded.

To the great satisfaction of the rest of the Division the Divisional Artillery had rejoined at the beginning of June, after their strenuous action on the Lys, and now covered the Division in the line.

About this time all three battalions of the 318th American Infantry Regiment were attached to the Division for instruction in the line.

A feature of the stationary warfare of these latter months

just previous to the great advance was the system of
Artillery " Crashes," or salvos, which was employed by
both sides ; these crashes were probably accountable for
far more casualties than any systematic bombardment in
such warfare, for they came whenever and wherever least
expected.

CHAPTER X.

THE GREAT ADVANCE.

From the Ancre to the Canal du Nord.

August and September, 1918.

FROM 19th July until 5th August the Division was in the Herissart area resting and training and held a Divisional Sports' Meeting, Horse Show and Race Meeting, all at Toutencourt.

On the latter date the Division went into the line again in the north and south of Aveluy Wood; during the absence of the Division the enemy had withdrawn to the eastern bank of the Ancre in consequence of successful operations of the 4th Army to the south; if he had not withdrawn the intention was that the Division should drive him back at any rate from the ground south of Aveluy Wood, and all preparations had been made for this operation.

On August 8th the 4th Army definitely assumed the offensive to the south of Albert with such success that it was decided by higher authorities to attempt to drive the enemy back from his commanding positions on the Thiepval ridge, north of Albert.

The two divisions of the 5th Corps in the line at this time were the 38th, on the right, and the 21st on the left.; the 18th Division of the 3rd Corps were on our right and we were soon to be thrown into very close touch with them and any other division which would relieve them during our long advance from the Ancre to beyond the Sambre.

The problem was a difficult one ; Albert and its crossings were held by the enemy ; his position to the north of Albert commanded ours and the Ancre was flooded to a width of 200 to 300 yards and there were no bridges.

The plan of attack was that the 113th Brigade should cross at Albert and the 114th Brigade opposite Hamel and that both these brigades should make a converging advance on Pozieres, leaving a gap between them of nearly three miles and a triangular space occupied by the enemy : this ground was to be dealt with later by the 115th Brigade who were also to support 113th Brigade.

This plan was duly carried out in the following manner : On the night of the 21st/22nd August six sections of the 14th Welsh under 2nd Lieut. I. Williams effected a crossing near Hamel and established themselves on the southern edge of Thiepval Wood, where they hung on against all attacks until reinforced later, on the night of the 23rd. A brother officer, 2nd Lieut. L. O. Griffiths, took it upon himself to ration the post so formed and in order to do so had to swim the river several times.

On the night of the 22nd/23rd August " A " and " B " Companies, of the 15th (Carmarthen Battalion) Welsh Regiment, under Capt. G. W. Lancaster and Lieut. Glyn Williams, crossed the Ancre near Hamel having to wade through water up to their chests under fire ; they then established themselves near St. Pierre Divion and maintained their position there the whole of the following day and night against repeated attacks. These gallant actions had far-reaching results.

On the night of the 22nd/23rd the 113th Brigade moved through Albert across the reconstructed bridges which were under continual shell fire and formed up within 100 yards of the enemy on a frontage of 450 yards, in the angle between the Albert-Bapaume Road and the Ancre ; in

E

order to do this it was necessary for both the attacking battalions to debouch from Albert by the Bapaume Road and then execute a flank movement to their left; this difficult manœuvre was successfully carried out, led by the 13th Royal Welsh Fusiliers the attack was launched at 4.45 a.m. on the 23rd against the hill one mile north-east of Albert, known as Unsa Hill : the position was captured and 194 prisoners, three guns and seven machine guns were taken.

The crossing of the 115th Brigade was made possible by the action of two small parties the next day (23rd). The site of the bridge at Aveluy where the 115th Brigade must cross was under fire from a spur to the south, where the enemy had two well known posts. Lieut. Connell of " A " Company, 13th Royal Welsh Fusiliers, after their successful attack that morning captured one of these posts and the seven machine guns in it. The other post was taken on by " A " Company, 2nd Royal Welsh Fusiliers, under 2nd Lieut. J. O. Smith, M.C., who made several attempts to cross the river and floods below Aveluy ; he at last found a way across, got his company across in small parties and eventually rushed the post, killing or capturing thirty of the enemy and taking eight machine guns.

The following night (23rd/24th) the two remaining companies of the 15th Welsh (Carmarthenshire Battalion) and the 14th Welsh (Swansea Battalion) joined the two companies of the 15th and the six sections of the 14th who had been holding on to their positions for over 36 hours ; the few existing foot bridges across the Ancre and the adjacent swamps had been repaired during the previous night and day by the 123rd Field Company, R.E., under continuous rifle fire, but during the crossing these bridges broke down and the majority of the 14th had to wade, in some cases up to their necks ; while they were forming up for attack on the eastern bank they were themselves counter-attacked by the enemy, but drove them off.

Meanwhile two battalions of the 115th Brigade had crossed the Ancre at Aveluy, over a bridge made by the 151st Field Company, R.E., under the supervision of Lieuts. Denning and Butler, and formed up on a one battalion frontage on the left of 113th Brigade.

At 1 a.m. the attack was launched and the 114th Brigade stormed the heights and took Thiepval ; the 113th Brigade had some hard fighting around La Boisselle and the 115th Brigade near Ovillers ; the subsequent advance of the 114th Brigade was not quite so strongly opposed and the bulk of the prisoners fell to them and the mopping-up battalion of the 115th Brigade.

By 4 p.m. the Division had reached a north and south line east of Ovillers and had captured in this day's operations 634 prisoners and 143 machine guns.

The following night all the Field Artillery (which included the 62nd Divisional Artillery) succeeded in crossing the Ancre over bridges made by the 123rd and 151st Field Companies, R.E., preparatory to supporting a further advance, and during the evening of the 24th the 113th Brigade pushed on and took Contalmaison and the other two Brigades reached Pozieres.

General Rhys Pryce had a narrow escape this evening on his entry into Contalmaison ; a pocket of the enemy had been overlooked by our troops on the high ground just west of the site of the village and opened a heavy fire on the Brigadier and his headquarters as they were riding along the road about 400 yards away.

During this attack on Contalmaison 2nd Lieut. K. R. T. Low, with No. 1 Section " C " Machine Gun Company, captured a post of thirty-five men and two machine guns by engaging the post from the front with his guns while half the section worked round the flank acting as Infantry.

The following day (25th) after practically no rest the Division advanced with all three brigades in line closely followed by the Artillery ; the enemy were found to be

holding in strength the line Mametz Wood—the site of
Bazentin le Petit Village—Bois des Foureaux (known by
the British as " High Wood " since the days of the Somme
battles of 1916).

After some stiff fighting the 113th Brigade captured
Mametz Wood, the 2nd Royal Welsh Fusiliers and 10th
South Wales Borderers captured Bazentin le Petit, and
the 14th and 15th Welsh captured the heights south of
Martinpuich but found " High Wood " so strongly held
and in such a commanding position that no impression
could be made upon it until the 113th and 115th Brigades
should make a further advance.

In order to launch this attack on Bazentin le Petit the
115th Brigade had to march to their assembly position by
compass bearing across open and very broken country in
the pitch dark ; this march was led by Lieut.-Col. Cock-
burn, and the whole brigade reached their allotted positions punctually at dawn.

The 114th Brigade were in a very difficult position for
the remainder of this day and night, for their line was
commanded by the enemy's position at High Wood and
they were counter-attacked several times.

The advance was continued the next day (26th) and the
113th Brigade with the 2nd Royal Welsh Fusiliers attached, fought their way against stubborn resistance across
the broken and hilly country, up to the western edge of
the site of the village of Longueval. This attack was
materially assisted by our machine guns and notably by
2nd Lieut. G. R. Waller who, with his section, was responsible for the surrender of a post of thirty of the enemy.

Another post which was holding up the attack was
bombarded by the 115th Trench Mortar Battery to such
good purpose that the garrison of the post, numbering
thirty-seven (all that were left alive), surrendered.

After reaching the outskirts of Longueval the 113th
Brigade were heavily counter-attacked throughout the

day by the enemy who could mass unseen in Delville
Wood, but the troops used their rifles with such success
and were so ably supported by the Artillery that all these
counter-attacks failed ; a message received from the front
line at this time read : " Have beaten off several counter-
attacks ; musketry training during last period of rest has
proved invaluable."

" D " Company of the 16th Royal Welsh Fusiliers,
under Capt. W. A. Paine, especially distinguished themselves by holding on to what they had won although both
flanks were exposed. The casualties of the Brigade this
day were seven officers and 720 other ranks.

Meanwhile, the 115th Brigade pushed along the valley
which runs to the south of High Wood and surrounded
those of the enemy there (fifteen machine guns and forty
men) who had not already retired in face of this cleverly
executed enveloping movement ; most of this work was
done by two companies of the 10th South Wales Borderers
under Capt. J. G. S. Hornsby and Capt. Hoffmeister, with
a loss of forty casualties. During this successful attack
the 115th Brigade received great assistance from an
attached troop of 20th Hussars.

The following morning at 4 a.m. the 114th Brigade
moved through the 115th Brigade and succeeded in reaching the Longueval-Flers road, and the 113th Brigade made
a slight advance but the enemy was holding the Longueval-
Delville Wood-Flers' position very strongly and nothing
further could be effected this day, except to hold on to
what we had won.

This was sufficiently difficult against the enemy's repeated attacks ; one of these was broken up by a brilliant
action by " D " Company of the 16th Royal Welsh Fusiliers, under 2nd Lieut. George, who saw the enemy forming
for attack and himself attacked them before their action
could develop ; he himself was killed just as his self-
imposed task was accomplished.

About 2 p.m. 122nd Brigade, Royal Field Artillery, was ordered to advance into action in the valley west of High Wood, in support of our Infantry who were advancing. Later it transpired that the enemy held the Longueval ridge in force. It was decided, however, to get the guns forward. There was only one possible route—the Bazentin-High Wood road which was narrow, made of planks, and in full view for 500 yards where it passed over the plateau between Bazentin and Martinpuich. One battery got through untouched but then two 5·9″ batteries were turned on to the road and put down a barrage 300 yards in depth, through which the remaining three batteries had to pass. This was accomplished by galloping down the road by sections at a time. There were direct hits on seven different teams, but the whole brigade got into action a few hundred yards west of High Wood. The limbers and teams passed back to the rear through the barrage which though now not so heavy caused further casualties. Shortly afterwards information was received that a strong hostile counter-attack was developing from the northern edge of Delville Wood. This was engaged by the brigade at 1000—1500 yards' range and definitely broken up. During this action the guns were under machine-gun fire from the right flank and also were engaged by a 77mm. battery which was in action just east of Longueval cross roads and firing over open sights and about 1500 yards' range causing many casualties.

Several further counter-attacks were made against the Infantry that evening but all were driven off by the combined fire of our Artillery and Infantry and of " B " and " D " Machine-Gun Companies.

The 28th was spent in bombarding the enemy's strong position and this would have allowed the Infantry to obtain a little rest but owing to heavy hostile shell fire this rest was practically negligible. Added to this the 113th Brigade towards the end of the day observed the enemy's resistance in Longueval to be weakening and by acting promptly on the initiative of the Brigadier drove him from the site of the village, and so completed the work which had been done by the Artillery throughout the day. In this they were ably and gallantly assisted by the Carabineers, who were under the command of the 113th Brigade this day, and were operating on their right flank.

Up to this date the Glamorgan Pioneers had been working day and night on repairing the approaches to the bridges across the Ancre and in improving communication generally ; it was owing to their work that it had been possible for the troops to be kept supplied with ammunition and rations during the rapid advance of the last three days. For it must be remembered that the enemy had blown craters in all important roads and had attempted to arrest our advance by all such methods. However, other troops were now found to take on this work and the Glamorgan Pioneers moved up to Bazentin as a fighting reserve to the Division.

One section of the 124th Field Company, R.E., had hitherto been attached to each Infantry Brigade but these were now withdrawn and concentrated at the same place. The remaining two Field Companies were still hard at work maintaining the bridges over the Ancre.

On the 29th the Division attacked and captured a position which had held out in 1916 for more than a month and which had been the scene of the most desperate fighting, that is the Ginchy ridge. The 113th Brigade took the actual site of the village moving by the south of Delville Wood, while the 115th Brigade passed through the 114th Brigade and advanced by the north of the wood ; the wood itself was cleared by the 13th Welsh Regiment.

The Machine Gun Battalion played a conspicuous part in this advance ; one company moving with each of the attacking brigades, while the remaining two companies covered the attack with a heavy barrage.

The advance continued throughout the day and in the evening the 10th South Wales Borderers captured Les Boeufs, and the 113th Brigade found themselves confronted by a strong force firmly established on a commanding position at Morval.

This day's advance by the Division was in the nature of an isolated movement, for the 18th Division on our right had orders merely to protect our right flank, and any advance of the 17th Division on our left was only dependent upon our success.

This evening the 113th Brigade made a determined effort to take Morval but without success and were relieved by the 114th Brigade during the night.

The 30th was a day of heavy fighting and casualties ; the enemy's resistance both by Infantry and Artillery was most determined and the 113th · Brigade, in reserve by Ginchy, and the reserve troops of the 115th Brigade, north of Delville Wood, and the Artillery on both sides of the wood were under continual shell fire throughout the day. Brigadier-General Hulke was severely wounded in the knee and Lt.-Col. Norman took command of the 115th Brigade.

Repeated attempts by the 114th Brigade to take Morval were unsuccessful.

The 31st was spent in bombarding the enemy's position.

During the period of this fighting there was of necessity an appreciable gap between the Division and the Division on our right and left and although touch was maintained no material assistance could be rendered by those divisions and consequently the Welsh Division was playing a lone hand. For the 18th Division had moved slightly southwards with the object of assisting our future advance on Sailly-Sallisel, by advancing towards that place from the south, and the 17th Division had Le Transloy for an objective and that fact tended to draw them away from us.

The plan of attack for the 1st September was as follows :

The 114th Brigade were to take Morval at all costs ; that done the 115th Brigade who were on their left were to capture Sailly-Sallisel and 113th Brigade were to move forward to support them.

At 4.45 a.m. all these battalions (much reduced in strength) of the 114th Brigade assaulted the Morval position and took it after desperate fighting, 200 enemy dead being counted on the ground.

The 115th Brigade then commenced their advance but the enemy were holding some commanding ground in the gap which existed between that brigade and the 17th Division on the left ; they thus came under heavy enfilade fire, the 2nd Royal Welsh Fusiliers on the left lost heavily, the 10th South Wales Borderers had to be turned aside to deal with the enemy and the advance of the 17th Royal Welsh Fusiliers was consequently unsupported. Thereupon the 113th Brigade was ordered to carry out the attack on Sailly Sallisel.

The final orders for this could not reach this Brigade until 1hr. 40min. before the attack was to be launched, but in spite of this it commenced punctually to time and was a complete success. The artillery barrage had to be fired in three parts and part one was actually being fired before the orders for part three reached the batteries. The Divisional Artillery fired this day over 1000 rounds per gun.

Two hundred and ninty-six prisoners were taken this day, a large percentage of whom were captured by the 16th Royal Welsh Fusiliers. This was an arduous day especially for the 113th Brigade, who were on the move from 2.15 a.m. till 10 p.m.

Thanks to their success it was possible to manœuvre troops by daylight in the hollow ground unseen between Morval and Sailly-Sallisel, and the 115th Brigade formed up for attack in this ground on the afternoon of the 2nd and attacked through the 113th Brigade ; but the latter troops were so mixed up with the enemy on the site of the village that our Artillery were prevented from giving adequate support to this attack which consequently failed.

About this time it was reported from higher authority that it was the intention of the enemy to reinforce those troops opposed to us by four divisions ; it was therefore anticipated that the Division might be thrown on to the defensive against superior numbers ; arrangements were made for this and one brigade of Artillery was slightly withdrawn so that the Artillery formed two echelons, two brigades in each echelon.

This was, however, the only alteration made in the actual disposition of troops, for patrols during the night discovered the enemy had withdrawn, and both 113th and 115th Brigades advanced at daybreak to an old German trench system running southwards from Mesnil en Arrouaise to Martin Wood.

During the afternoon the 114th Brigade passed through them and their advanced troops occupied Manancourt and Etricourt, after some fighting in which they were ably supported by " B " and " C " Batteries, 122nd Brigade, commanded by Major A. C. Saville, M.C., and Major A. D. C. Clarke, M.C. These batteries advanced close in rear of the leading Infantry and came into action east of St. Martin's Wood, while the enemy were stiil that side of the Canal.

In order to do this they had to advance across the open in full view for a considerable distance and during this advance three of the twelve guns were hit.

All bridges across the Canal du Nord were found to be destroyed and the enemy was holding the further bank in strength. During the next forty-eight hours the enemy smothered the Canal valley with gas shell which made operations very difficult and costly.

The canal is here an impassable obstacle, and it looked as if the advance might be checked for some time had it

not been for one of the most brilliant Infantry actions of
the Advance, which was performed by the 13th Welsh
Regiment the next day, under the personal direction of
Major Hobbs.

The enemy had machine guns on the bank but not
covering the actual water ; noticing this, Major Hobbs
rushed a platoon down to an old trench on the near bank,
from which a ditch led down towards the *debris* of the
Etricourt road bridge ; here the platoon engaged the
attention of the nearest machine guns and one section
crawled down the ditch across the fallen bridge and up
the far bank ; crawling on their stomachs this section
advanced to within charging distance of the nearest
machine gun, then leapt up and bayonetted the gunners ;
they were quickly joined by the remainder of the platoon
and a bridgehead was formed which enabled the remainder
of the company (under Capt. Beech, M.C.) to cross.

Similar action took place at Manancourt where a company of the 14th Welsh Regiment, led by Major J. A.
Daniels, D.S.O., M.C., of the 15th Welsh (attached to the
14th) crossed, and each of these battalions had thus one
company across by 11.30 a.m. ; these companies cleared
the eastern bank of the enemy and then pushed forward
to cover · the crossing of the remainder of the Brigade,
which was effected with the help of the 123rd Field Company, R.E., by 5 p.m. This Field Company worked continuously throughout the afternoon and night and the
following day ; they were under shell fire the whole time,
and had to perform the whole of the work in gas masks ;
and sustained thirty casualties ; it was owing to their
efforts that our relief by the 21st Division the following
night and their subsequent advance was made possible.

During the day (September 4th) the remainder of the
Divisional Artillery advanced in close support and came
into action on the forward slopes south of Mesnil ; in order
to do this they also had to move across the open from

Sailly Sallisel in full view from the enemy's position about Equancourt ; that such a movement was possible without prohibitive casualties is probably due to the action of the 17th Division on our left, which was engaging part of the enemy's attention at the time. A section of " D " Machine Gun Company crossed this ground at the gallop this day in order to reinforce the remainder of the machine guns which had either moved forward by night or had been carried forward by hand.

All guns and vehicles approaching our forward troops had to move through Sailly Sallisel as being the only road ; the site of this village was under continual shell fire and it speaks well for the march discipline of artillery and transport that nothing in the nature of a block ever occured in the traffic.

On the 5th September the Division was relieved by the 21st Division and withdrew into Corps reserve at Le Transloy, Les Boefs and Delville Wood, where they were accommodated in tents and in any huts which remained more or less intact after the recent fighting. These huts were partly English and partly German for this country had changed hands three times since 1916. There was of course not the vestige of a house remaining to be seen in this area.

The Artillery remained in action but the remainder of the Division now had six days' badly needed rest, for they had been continuously engaged for more than a fortnight, during which time they had driven the enemy back step by step, fighting hard the whole way for a distance of 15 miles ; they had captured twenty-nine officers, 1,886 other ranks, six guns and many machine guns, and had suffered 3,614 casualties.

Brig.-General H. de Pree, C.B., C.M.G., took over command of the 115th Brigade.

During this period the Divisional Artillery (with the 62nd Artillery attached) had been continuously on the move in close support of the Infantry and had fired over three hundred thousand rounds.

Supply difficulties during this period were a severe tax on the energy of the Divisional Train and Mechanical Transport Company. The railhead remained for sometime at Ferme Rosel, near the Amiens-Doullens road, and was never further forward than Aveluy even when the troops were east of Canal du Nord. This meant long journeys for both these units, especially for the train who were sometimes obliged to use bye roads and tracks in order to leave the main roads clear for the supply of ammunition.

CHAPTER XI.

THE GREAT ADVANCE.

From the Canal du Nord to the Selle.

September and October, 1918.

WHEN the time came for us to relieve the 17th Division on
the 11th September it was found that the whole line was
held up in front of Gouzeaucourt, where the enemy were
making a determined resistance ; we were here opposed
by a Jaegar division who fought with great stubbornness.
The front line was taken over by the 115th Brigade and
occupied what had been the support trench of a system
which had been dug by the British in 1917, when they
were brought up against the celebrated Hindenberg Line ;
the enemy occupied what had been the front trench of
this system ; this system ran along a ridge from Epehy
to Trescault almost overlooking the Scheldt Canal and it
was for this reason apparently that the enemy were holding
on so desperately to this high ground, though other (strategical) reasons apart from local considerations of ground
made it imperative for him to hold this ground and the
Hindenberg Line as long as .possible. The 113th Brigade
held what had been the reserve trench of this system near
Dessart Wood and the 114th Brigade occupied what had
been a strong German defensive trench system near
Equancourt.

The Division Headquarters moved forward to some old
huts at Etricourt (made in 1917 as Headquarters of 4th

Corps) and this proved to be a most undesirable residence, for the German high velocity gun had the line of the Canal taped to a nicety and their aeroplanes used to bomb the ruined villages and huts along the canal on most nights.

No further advance was made until the 18th, but the Division had anything but a quiet time during this period ; the enemy made repeated attempts to drive us off the ridge and our front line and support troops and Artillery positions were throughout subjected to a heavy fire from his artillery in which he was especially strong at this time.

Preparatory to attacking the enemy the 114th Brigade and the 113th Brigade came up into the front line and 115th Brigade withdrew into reserve.

The attack commenced at 5.40 a.m. on the 18th September, and the 114th Brigade on the right were completely successful and reached a position south of Gouzeaucourt ; the enemy, however, maintained his hold on this ruined village and the Corps on our left were not intended to attack, consequently the advance of the 113th Brigade was met by flanking fire from the north and their left battalion suffered severely, losing eleven out of the twelve officers who went into action.

The 14th Royal Welsh Fusiliers were on the right of this Brigade and " A " and " D " companies reached their objective in front of Gouzeaucourt but they were by that time much reduced in strength, their left was completely in the air and there was a considerable gap between them and the 114th Brigade on the right ; nevertheless these two companies under 2nd Lieut. J. Evans held on in this position till 4 p.m. the next day, and during that time beat off seven counter-attacks.

The left flank of the 114th Brigade was thus exposed but was protected by the initiative of Lieut. H. Nellis, of the Machine Gun Battalion, who supported by 2nd Lieut. G. E. Lowe, M.C., and " A " Company 15th Welsh, pushed his guns forward and with them broke up at least one counter-attack. Later he noticed a party of about fifty of the enemy collecting in a sunken road to his front : on these he advanced single handed and caused half of them to surrender ; the remainder however seeing that they had to deal with one man only scattered into the open and commenced shooting at him ; but his own guns dealt with these and he brought in his prisoners.

The casualties in officers had been heavy and two companies of the 13th Welsh were eventually under the command of C. S. M. Williams, M.M., who was largely instrumental in the protection of the flank of the Brigade.

After the 114th Brigade had gained their position conspicuous service was done by three officers who succeeded in visiting the whole Brigade front at different times in spite of continuous machine gun and sniping fire ; these officers were Capt. G. C. Bucknall, M.C. (Brigade Major), Capt. D. L. Prestage, M.C., and Lieut. Minshull, M.C.

A remarkable achievement was performed by Lieut. W. A. White, of the Machine Gun Battalion, during this attack ; he is credited with the capture of two separate machine guns and the destruction of their teams single handed ; he later rushed a hostile rifle post with a handful of men and towards the end of the day he materially assisted in defeating a German counter-attack by turning their own machine gun on to them. He was awarded the V.C. for these actions.

The left of the 113th Brigade made repeated attempts to get forward ; after the first attempt had failed all available artillery was turned on to the objective for thirty minutes ; this was done twice and after each bombardment the Infantry succeeded in reaching the position, but each time the enemy's fire from the flank was so intense that the position was quite untenable.

During this operation and the previous week our casualties had been heavy and the Division was withdrawn into reserve on the 20th and occupied the trenches near Equancourt, huts near Rocquigny and tents near Le Transloy. The Artillery as usual remained in action.

The remainder of the Division now had a week's rest and had an opportunity of absorbing any drafts that had arrived as reinforcements.

The Corps was now up against the celebrated Hindenberg Line and the 4th Army on our right was similarly opposed. Reconnaissance showed that the strength of this line had not been exaggerated ; it was moreover protected by the Scheldt Canal as far south as Bony ; it was also known that the enemy had a strong defensive system running north and south by Villers Outreaux, known as the Masnieres-Beaurevoir line.

The plan of attack was that the 4th Army should assault south of Bony and that the 2nd American Corps which had lately joined the 4th Army should then turn northwards, while part of the 4th Army secured the crossings at Vendhuille.

Consequently the Division had to be prepared for three different lines of action ; that is either to relieve the American troops and continue their northward advance, or to relieve the 4th Army troops at Vendhuille or to assist in a frontal attack against the Hindenberg Line.

In order to be prepared therefore the Division moved on the 28th September into old trenches near Sorel le Grand and Hendicourt ; both these villages were completely ruined and gave practically no cover ; the Division remained ready to move at two hours' notice until October 3rd, when the success of the 4th Army made it necessary for the Division to move in a south-easterly direction in order to fulfil the first of the three roles mentioned above.

This necessitated a flank march across the enemy's front over ground, parts of which the enemy could see, and the whole of which was under continual shell fire and infested by gas.

This move was carried out in two bounds and during

F

the second (on the 4th October) the 115th Brigade with
the 151st Field Company, R.E., and " A " Company
Machine Gun Battalion, reached Bony and that night
relieved the troops of the 50th Division, who had carried
out the operation intended for the 105th American Regiment and had occupied the high ground north of Le Catelet
facing north ; this relief was a difficult one, for the situation was complicated and the troops had great difficulty
in finding their way.

The great Hindenberg Line thus being turned the enemy
slowly withdrew to the Masnieres-Beaurevoir line, and all
the energy and skill of the Royal Engineers and Pioneers
were called into play in order to bridge the Canal, improve
the approaches and get the guns across at Ossus ; the
124th Field Company and the whole of the Glamorgan
Pioneers were employed on this work with such good
results that the whole of the Divisional Artillery (who had
been supporting the 33rd Division) and the 33rd Divisional
Artillery and the 34th Army Brigade, R.F.A., were got
across and into action on the far side during that day.

The enemy's position was found to be very strongly
entrenched and wired, being indeed a part of the Hindenberg system, and the next two days were spent in reconnaissance and in bringing up heavy artillery and in making
good a " jumping off " line for our next attack, running
north and south through Aubencheul ; 115th and 113th
Brigades were on this line and 114th Brigade was in support in the Hindenburg Line south of La Terriere.

October 8th perhaps saw the stiffest fighting of the whole
advance.

The task imposed upon the Division entailed an advance
of over five thousand yards through a very strong position ;
this involved the employment of the whole Division and
a plan of attack which was of necessity slightly complicated ; owing to the necessity of co-ordinating our attack
with that of the divisions on the flanks and the fact that

their plans could not be made longer in advance, the orders
could not be issued to brigadiers before 3 p.m. on the 7th,
and then only verbally ; the attack was to commence at
1 a.m. the next morning and the night was very dark and
wet.

The plan was as follows :—

At 1 a.m. the 10th South Wales Borderers and 17th
Royal Welsh Fusiliers were to attack by the south and
north of Villers Outreaux respectively while the 2nd Royal
Welsh Fusiliers, in brigade reserve, were to deal with the
village itself at daybreak assisted by two tanks.

The 16th Royal Welsh Fusiliers on the right and the
13th Royal Welsh Fusiliers on the left were to form the
attacking line of the 113th Brigade and advance through
Mortho Wood and by the south of it.

The objective of these attacks was a trench line running
north and south just east of Villers Outreaux.

The 114th Brigade was to form up on this line and
continue the attack at 8 a.m., and in the meantime the
whole of the 38th and 33rd Divisional Artillery and the
38th Machine Gun Battalion were to move forward in
order to support them.

The outstanding features of the action as it was fought
were that the 115th Brigade failed in their first attempt
but re-organised and completely succeeded the second
time, that the 113th Brigade attack was in consequence
held up and 114th Brigade consequently had to fight their
way to their assembly position, and that owing to the un-
certainty of the situation the Artillery only had one and
a half hours in which to change position and open fire in
support of the 114th Brigade.

The first attack of the 10th South Wales Borderers was
delayed and thrown into confusion by unseen wire and
machine-gun fire and it was necessary to re-organise before
the attack could be renewed ; during this first attack
C.S.M. Williams, D.C.M., M.M., of " B " Company, seeing

that his men were held up by fire from a machine-gun post ordered a Lewis gun to engage the post while he, accompanied by one man, went forward and took prisoners the garrison of eleven ; for this and for further conspicuous skill and gallantry this day he was awarded the V.C.

While this was in progress the 17th Royal Welsh Fusiliers were having desperate fighting to the north of the main road ; here again unseen wire was encountered ; wire which was under a murderous fire from machine guns in the trench beyond ; determined attempts were made by both first and second lines to get through this wire, the first two companies alone losing ten officers and 120 men. All attempts failed and the Battalion withdrew and reorganised preparatory to trying again.

Meanwhile the 113th Infantry Brigade broke through the enemy's line, the 16th Royal Welsh Fusiliers reaching Angelus orchard whence they were unable to progress further. The 13th Royal Welsh Fusiliers on the left managed to get further thanks mainly to Captain Wynne Edwards, D.S.O., M.C., who during a personal reconnaissance the day before had found two gaps in the enemy's wire.

Such was the situation at daybreak when the 114th Brigade were already advancing expecting to be able to move unmolested to their forming-up place beyond Villers Outreaux ; it had already been decided to postpone their actual attack till 11.30 a.m., but not in time to prevent them moving, and when these troops arrived between Villers Outreaux and Mortho Wood they found themselves involved in desperate fighting in support of the 113th Brigade.

Meanwhile the two leading battalions of the 115th Brigade had been preparing for a second assault and an incentive to this was given by the arrival of the 2nd Royal Welsh Fusiliers and two other tanks at dawn. There had been no time to warn this Battalion of the altered situation and they, like the 114th Brigade, found the conditions entirely different from what they expected ; Lt.-Col. Norman at once issued fresh orders to his Battalion and it is perhaps not too much to say that their action was chiefly responsible for the success of the whole day's work. He formed up " A " and " B " Companies for attack and allotted the tanks to " B " with orders to break through the enemy's trench line at all costs.

The 17th Royal Welsh Fusiliers led by Lt.-Col. Beasley in person formed upon their left. Their attack was materially assisted by the enterprise of Major A. D. C. Clarke, D.S.O., M.C., who was commanding C/122nd battery and who while awaiting the order to move his battery forward had come up into the front line and brought a telephone wire with him ; from here he not only reported the situation but directed the fire of his own battery into the enemy's trench. Aided by this and by the Tanks, " B " Company, 2nd Royal Welsh Fusiliers, under Capt. Kirkby, D.S.O., succeeded in breaking through and were quickly followed by " C " Company ; the former went straight forward and the latter turned right-handed and cleared the way for the advance of the rest of the battalion.

This success was quickly followed up by the machine guns under Lieut. E. A. Evans, and his skilful handling of his own and captured guns materially assisted the advance of our extreme left where two battalions of the 114th Brigade had now taken up the running. They had succeeded in fighting their way up to the Villers Outreaux-Lesdain road but here came under heavy fire from a chateau, just east of Mont Ecouvez (known as Chateau d'Angles), which was eventually rushed by " A " Company of the 15th Welsh under Lieut. Richards.

It was now eleven o'clock and the action of the 115th Brigade had had effect and the 114th Brigade were enabled to reach their forming-up place by the time that our

70 A History of the

creeping barrage opened for their attack ; the 13th Welsh had followed up the second and successful attack of the 10th South Wales Borderers on the south side of the village and formed for attack on the right of the 14th Welsh, who were in the centre of the 114th Brigade line.

The Artillery were only just up in time for this attack ; up till 10 a.m. the situation had been so obscure that the guns could not be allowed to go forward, but by 11.30 eleven out of the sixteen batteries were in action near Villers Outreaux and the remaining five came into action there ten minutes later.

The attack of the 114th Brigade once launched progressed rapidly and resulted in a complete rout of the enemy and by the afternoon the line of the Premont-Esnes road (the final objective) was reached ; the 114th Brigade had thus been fighting for twelve hours. The Artillery was again moved forward and some of the batteries came into action east of Malincourt, 9000 yards east of the positions which they occupied at the beginning of the action.

The 114th Brigade continued to hold this line throughout the night until the 33rd Division passed through them the next morning : while the 113th Brigade remained in support and 115th Brigade went into billets in Villers Outreaux. This was the first time that the troops had entered or seen an inhabitable house since leaving rest billets on the 4th August.

Our captures this day were seven officers, 373 other ranks, twenty guns (including one eight inch howitzer) and many machine guns.

Our casualties were sixty-nine officers and 1,221 other ranks.

All the wounded were cleared by the following morning by the Field Ambulances.

At this time our railhead had reached Fins and the Divisional Train was in the neighbourhood of Epehy and had hard work to feed the troops in their new positions, but worse was to happen to 330th Company next day, for the 33rd Division took up the pursuit of the enemy and our Artillery went forward in support of them, consequently the Company had to deliver to the waggon lines east of Clary, had to do so under fire and did not finish delivering till 11 p.m., having left the refilling point at 8 a.m. The Company then had to return to Aubencheul, where it arrived next morning, having performed a march of 40 miles during the twenty-four hours.

At Clary we reached the zone inhabited by the civil population who gave us a great reception after four years of German rule ; every house in these villages produced a tricolour flag which must have been carefully hidden away during these four years. The troops soon learnt that a white flag denoted the absence of the enemy but unfortunately the enemy soon learnt this too.

It was now the role of the Division to keep close up behind the 33rd Division ready to relieve or pass through them when required. This was done with such effect that the leading Division complained of being continually " bumped."

The Divisional Artillery meanwhile was co-operating with the leading Division and on the early morning of October 10th the batteries of the 122nd Brigade, R.F.A., moved forward on the heels of the 7th Cavalry Brigade, and in front of the British Infantry (33rd Division). The three 18-pounder batteries of the Brigade came into action north of the Le Cateau-Cambrai road, 3000 yards w.n.w. of Le Cateau, and were of material use in driving the enemy across the river. At about midday, before the west bank of the Selle had been cleared of the enemy, C/122nd under Major A. D. C. Clarke was moved forward another 1000 yards. The battery had to move across a ridge in full view of the enemy, and as the leading section surmounted the crest, it came under heavy shell fire from the enemy and almost at the outset the firing battery waggon of No.1 Sub-section became a casualty, the wheel driver and his horses being killed by a shell.

When about 200 yards down the forward slope of the crest, the hand wheeler on No. 1 Gun team tripped up while at the gallop, and fell, bringing the whole team to a standstill in full view of the enemy and under heavy shell fire.

Rapidly grasping the situation and with great coolness under heavy fire the section commander, 2nd Lieut. J. C. Parsons dismounted himself and all but the lead driver, and with remarkable rapidity succeeded in extricating the fallen horse, righting the team and thus getting his gun into action with the least possible delay. While the enemy's artillery was being attracted by this stationary target the centre and rear section having cleared the crest at a gallop got safely into action.

This battery then did splendid work against columns of enemy transport and troops retiring eastwards up and over the high ground around Forest. The battery was able to engage targets quite out of range of the batteries in rear and maintained its position all day and in the face of heavy fire.

The enemy, however, were found to have a very strong position on the eastern bank of the river (Selle). The leading Division attacked this position on the 12th and succeeded in crossing the river but at a great cost in casualties, so much so that they were eventually obliged to withdraw.

It was now decided to call a halt on the western bank and the Division closed up to Troisvilles and Bertry preparatory to relieving the 33rd Division ; this relief was carried out on the night of the 13/14th by the 115th Brigade. 114th Brigade remaining in support at Troisvilles and 113th Brigade in reserve at Bertry.

The opposing sides were now facing each other across

the Selle which here runs in a valley, the sides of which form glacis-like slopes ; it was impossible for even single men to move on these slopes in daylight without drawing fire.   The enemy from now onwards appeared to be very strong in artillery and used it with effect.

On the 16th he bombarded the gun positions of the whole of 121st Brigade with gas shell for eight hours.

The period from the 14th to the 20th was spent in reconnoitring for crossings, bringing up heavy artillery, and preparing footbridges ready for placing across the river.

This latter work was entrusted to the 123rd Field Company, R.E., under Major Pressy, M.C., and by the time that the attack commenced twenty-four footbridges and one tank bridge had been placed across the river and the approaches to them had been marked by tape ; this was a work of considerable difficulty for, except on our left-centre we had no posts across the river, so that the work had to be done in front of our outpost line ; in some places it was possible to launch those bridges beforehand and leave them concealed, but in others the bridges had to be carried down on the night of and the night before the attack. The company had only thirty-five men available for this work and they were employed on it for seventy-four hours out of the ninety-six.

They were loud in their praise of the assistance given them by a carrying party of the 17th Royal Welsh Fusiliers.

So successful were these bridging operations that when the time came it was found that the railway embankment on the far side was a much greater natural obstacle than the river itself.

The night of the attack, 19/20th, was very wet and this embankment was so slippery as to be almost impassable, it was heavily wired and protected by innumerable machine guns.

The position was formidable and the enemy intended to hold it at all costs, one reason being that it was the best one on which to oppose us and the other (not apparent till later) that from that high ground beyond the Selle a view could be obtained as far as Mormal Forest. A French civilian informed us that from what he knew of the country he was sure that we should never drive the enemy from this ground.

The 113th Brigade attacked with all three battalions in the line, the 114th had the 13th on the right and the 14th on the left and the 15th in close support.

Two battalions of the 115th Brigade were brought forward from Troisvilles to hold the ground this side of the river in case of a strong counter-attack.

All attacking battalions except the 13th Welsh had to form up on our side of the river and cross in battle formation. One tank accompanied each brigade and crossed the river but soon afterwards became stuck in the mud.

The fighting for the railway was desperate but it was carried well up to time (2.30 a.m.) and the rear waves passed through on their way to assault the high ground beyond. The capture of the railway on the right was largely due to the successful action of the 16th Royal Welsh Fusiliers on the extreme right, under Major Dale, D.S.O., M.C. : they were the first to obtain a footing on the railway and turned left-handed taking some of the enemy's machine guns in rear. The 14th Welsh had difficulty in crossing and this was only made possible by the preliminary reconnaissance carried out by Lieut. Gundrey, M.C.

As soon as they were across, they came under heavy enfilade fire from a position which swept the whole valley ; this they rushed and were ready to assault the railway as soon as our barrage should lift.

Here a large share in the fighting was taken by " B " Company of the 19th Welsh Pioneers, under 2nd Lieuts. W. H. Brace, D.C.M., and R. H. Pugh, M.M., who were attached to the 114th Brigade mainly for the purpose of assisting in the consolidation of the final objective ; they. however, joined in the assault on the railway and were not only largely instrumental in capturing this position but passed on with the Infantry and are credited with the capture of a German battery on the heights beyond while the latter were firing at the advancing Infantry ; in this action Sergeant Murphy killed three of the enemy single handed and captured fifteen more.

This holiday work of the Pioneers did not however interfere with their role of consolidation later on, which they carried out with good effect, helping the Infantry to dig themselves in and so resist the several determined counter-attacks which endeavoured to drive them off the position that evening and night.

During this action " B " Company of the 15th Welsh (now under Capt. J. G. Owen, M.C.) repeated their performance of the Ancre ; their bridges had not been able to stand the strain of bearing more than the front line. and this company found them all broken but continued their advance by wading ; the depth of the water at this point was measured by the fact that every man's respirator (worn on the chest) was wet through.

The whole of our line remained unmoved on the final objective throughout the next two days when the 33rd Division passed through us on the evening of the 22nd.

We captured during these operations 212 prisoners. a battery of field guns. three trench mortars, and forty machine guns, while 225 enemy dead were counted on the ground.

The success of the attack was largely due to the extreme accuracy of the Artillery barrage.

During the evacuation of our wounded some extraordinarily good work was done by 131st Field Ambulance under the supervision of Major W. D. Frew.

During the early part of this period the Divisional Train was at Villers Outreaux and were feeding the troops at

Troisvilles, the railhead being still at Fins, and at this time influenza was rampant among the *personnel* of the train and two companies of the train were without any officers at all.

On the 21st the whole of the Divisional Artillery crossed the Selle by temporary bridges made by the Royal Engineers : the line of the river and railway was naturally a target for the enemy's guns, and the result was that the Engineers suffered considerable casualties while making these bridges (especially 124th Field Company), and the guns when in position on the far side had to undergo a continual bombardment before and during the subsequent attack by the 33rd Division on the 23rd.

In these positions they were within 500 yards of the enemy's Infantry and so could not move further forward.

CHAPTER XII.

THE GREAT ADVANCE.

From the Selle to beyond the Sambre.

October and November, 1918.

DURING the four days which followed the 22nd October the Division again had to keep close to the 33rd Division, and again the same " complaint " was heard ; the troops were moved gradually forward through the villages of Forest and Croix but this main road was so constantly shelled by a numerous artillery that the troops slept in the open, well away from all villages.

Early on the morning of the 26th the 33rd Division captured Englefontaine and the Welsh Division relieved them there the same day preparatory to a further advance.

We were now confronted by the Mormal Forest, said to be the third largest forest in France, and considerable opposition was expected ; the line therefore remained stationary until November 4th to give time for preparation ; but the strategical situation elsewhere on the front and the fact that we were within striking distance of Mauberge, an important point on the enemy's line of communication, made it desirable not to delay longer than was imperative.

In the meantime our line, especially the supports and battery positions were subjected to an almost continuous bombardment. The enemy attempted a counter-attack against the 17th Royal Welsh Fusiliers, for which the

latter retaliated by rounding up all the enemy in the outlying houses of Englefontaine to a distance of 500 yards
from our position and bringing back twenty-four prisoners
and six machine guns : in this action they were ably
assisted by the 115th Trench Mortar Battery, part of whom
were acting as Infantry.

There were at first many civilian inhabitants in Poix du
Nord and Englefontaine but the shelling became so heavy
that it was necessary to evacuate them ; the enemy also
at first occupied many of the outlying houses of Englefontaine and in many places the opposing sides occupied
adjacent houses, while the inhabitants lived in the cellars
of each. The enemy were evacuated by such means as
described above.

During this period No. 330 Company of the Divisional
Train were unlucky in receiving five bombs dropped from
an aeroplane while they were refilling during darkness ;
all horses stampeded, but all the waggons were pulled up
and brought back by their drivers without further accident.

The final objective for the 4th November was the road
which runs north-east and south-east through the forest
from Les Grandes Patures ; there were three objectives,
the first being a line about 500 yards within the western
edge of the forest.

The plan was perfectly straightforward. The 115th
Brigade was to take the first objective, the 113th Brigade
the second, and the 114th Brigade the third. The execution of this plan was not so simple ; the Division was
attacking on a frontage of 2000 yards through trees and had
first to penetrate a series of very strongly-fenced orchards ;
the existence of the trees meant that the Infantry could
not keep nearly so close to our barrage as they would in
the open ; though the forest itself made it difficult to
maintain direction yet there were many open spaces within
it where the enemy could get a good field of fire against
our troops ; and, lastly, owing to the Division being con-

siderably in advance of the divisions on right and left our attack was not timed to commence until 45 minutes after theirs, so as to give them time to come up level with us.

The night before the attack General De Pree moved his headquarters into the village of Englefontaine and had hardly reached there when the enemy opened one of the heaviest bombardments ever experienced during the advance.

The attack next day was rather more than a success.

The 115th Brigade undoubtedly had the hardest fighting for the enemy were holding the edge of the forest in strength and at this hour of the morning (6.15 a.m.) there was a dense fog. The 2nd Royal Welsh Fusiliers had especially a difficult task for there was an unavoidable gap of 400 yards between them and the division on our right. " B " Company was on the extreme right and it was owing to the skilful leading of its commander, Capt. J. Butler, M.C., D.C.M., and the dash exhibited by his subordinates that the Company won through to its objective.

The 113th Brigade had formed up in assembly positions close to Englefontaine in order to be ready to follow up 115th Brigade closely and they had to run the gauntlet of the very heavy counter-bombardment put down by the enemy in and around this place. The 114th Brigade suffered from the same cause and had a long march up from the village of Forest.

In the case of every brigade the attack was made in lines of small columns, each column led by an officer marching by compass ; one of the results of attacking in this formation was that these columns were often able to pass by the enemy machine-gun posts and attack them from the rear.

Immediately after the second objective was taken by the 113th Brigade it became necessary for the Artillery to move forward ; this was done and the 114th Brigade gained their final objective well up to time just before dark.

The 13th Welsh who were on the left were ordered to push forward two companies at midnight through the forest to the line Sarbaras-la Tete Noir ; " A " and " B " companies, under Capt. H. Wilcoxon, M.C., and Capt. W. B. Morgan, M.C., moved forward with considerable difficulty as the night was very dark and it was raining hard ; the troops surrounded the above villages and took the enemy completely by surprise, capturing sixty-five of them ; they then sent forward strong patrols into Berliamont which reached there at about 7 a.m. ; these patrols marched straight into the town and proceeded to clear it of the enemy ; they captured a further sixty prisoners and handed it over clear of the enemy to the advance guard of the 33rd Division about an hour later. Thus the advance troops of the Division during the operations of the previous twenty-four hours had penetrated to a distance of about four miles further than the Divisions on the right and left and had overrun the line of the first objective of the next day's attack. These companies were on the move from 7 a.m. on the 4th till 7 a.m. on the 5th, during which time they had covered a distance of 11½ miles, the first half of which was traversed under shell fire and the second in continuous contact with the enemy.

The total captures by the Division during this twenty-four hours were eight officers, 522 other ranks, twenty-three guns and many machine guns, of which the 115th Brigade took over 200 prisoners and two guns.

On the 5th November the 33rd Division again passed through us and effected the crossing of the Sambre. From now onwards we had to contend with considerable difficulties in the matter of roads.

There were only two available for the whole Corps and these had been destroyed by the enemy in most methodical fashion.

The wounded numbering 411, were evacuated by the 131 Field Ambulance on the 4th and 5th by means of relays of bearers established through the forest. All the Field Companies and the Pioneers got to work at daybreak on the 5th and soon succeeded in making the roads sufficiently passable for Artillery, but the work was colossal and it was some days before any motor traffic could move through the forest.

On the 5th the Infantry of the Division remained on the captured positions ; it was a day of pouring rain and 113th and 114th Brigades could obtain practically no cover.

On the 6th 113th Brigade closed up near to the Sambre, and 115th Brigade took their place, and the Division was thus disposed when the order was received to relieve the 33rd Division the following day.

The 33rd Division had now reached Dourlers and two of our brigades were still in the forest and there was only one bridge available for the Division (at Berliamont) and that was being shelled, consequently this relief promised to be one of some difficulty, particularly as the 33rd Division were still pressing on and no one knew when or where they would stop. However, all three brigades were across the river by 4 p.m. and the 113th Brigade passed through the leading brigade of the 33rd Division by 10 p.m. that night and by dawn the next morning had reached the Avesnes-Mauberge road ; here it looked as if the enemy might possibly be going to make a stand and he seemed inclined to counter-attack the left of the 113th Brigade, which was some way advance of the neighbouring division, consequently the 114th Brigade who were in support near Ecuelin and " C " Squadron, Oxfordshire Hussars, who were with 113th Brigade had to watch this flank rather carefully, especially as the question of ammunition supply was so acute owing to the bad roads, that only a few batteries were in support.

However, during the next three days the 113th Brigade kept pushing on with gradually increasing speed and it looked as if the campaign would end in a running fight, finishing in Berlin, when the "cease fire," sounding at 11 a.m. on November 11th, found our advanced guard brigade headquarters at Wattignies la Victoire with their troops east of Dimechaux and with the attached cavalry and cyclists in touch with the enemy on the Belgian frontier near Hestrud.

Thus ended the Great Advance during which the Division had been fighting for two and a half months, had covered over sixty miles as the crow flies, had captured forty-five officers, 3,037 other ranks, 520 machine guns, fifty trench mortars and forty-three guns, and had lost 407 officers and 8,274 other ranks.

It is worthy of note that during the Advance the Divisional Artillery was in action the whole time except for a period of seventy-two hours.

CHAPTER XIII.

CONCLUSION.

THE Division now remained in and near Aulnoye until after Christmas and settled down to training and recreation. Competitions were inaugurated in every form of athletic sport and these continued so long as there were any men left in the Division to take part in them. But to the regret of everyone it was decided that the Division was not to form part of the Army of Occupation but was to be demobilised, and during December over 3000 miners left the Division to go home ; the demeanour of these men on their departure showed that even the prospect of returning to their homes did not overweigh their regret at leaving the Division and their comrades with whom they had fought through so many months.

On November 20th Brig.-General Rhys Pryce left to take up the appointment of Director-General of Mobilisation in India, after being with the Division for over three and a half years ; he was succeeded by Brig.-General Carton de Wiart, V.C., C.M.G., D.S.O.

On December 3rd the Division was honoured by a visit from His Majesty the King, who saw all the troops.

Immediately after Christmas the Division moved into huts and billets just east of Amiens, at Querrieu, Allenville, Warloy, and Glisy, and about this time the Divisional Rugby Football team went to Paris to play two matches against France, at the New Year ; in the first of these matches the Division was defeated but won the return match.

This same team easily won the 5th Corps' Cup and went home on February 28th to play several matches in Wales.

On the 16th January the King's Colour was presented to each Infantry Battalion of the Division (except the 2nd Royal Welsh Fusiliers).

His Royal Highness the Prince of Wales visited the Division, staying at Divisional Headquarters from the 5th to the 8th February. He spent all the hours of daylight among the troops, and during that time visited every unit in the Division.

ORDERS, DECORATIONS AND MEDALS, ETC., AWARDED TO THE DIVISION.

1st December, 1915, to 1st March, 1919.

V.C.	5
C.B.	3
C.M.G.	14
2nd Bar to D.S.O.	2
D.S.O. (bar)	7
D.S.O.	77
O.B.E.	3
M.B.E.	1
2nd Bar to M.C.	3
Bar to M.C.	33
M.C.	411
Albert Medal, 1st Class	1
Albert Medal, 2nd Class	1
Bar to D.C.M.	2
D.C.M.	252
Bar to M.M.	52
M.M.	1098
M.S.M.	147
Promotion to rank of Major-General	1
Brevet-Colonel	3
Brevet-Lieut.-Colonel	7
Brevet-Major	3
Mention in Despatches	453
Chevalier de Legion d'honnour	2
Medaille Militaire	5
Croix de Guerre (French and Belgian)	69
Italian Silver Medal	1
Italian Bronze Medal	5
Decoration Militaire (Belgian)	1
Montenegrin Silver Medal for Merit	1
Commandeur de l'Order de Leopold	1
Total	**2,664**

TOTAL CASUALTIES

During the time the Division was in France.

OFFICERS.			OTHER RANKS.		
K.	W.	M.	K.	W.	M.
275	1009	39	4144	22259	1654

1846549R0006

Printed in Great Britain
by Amazon.co.uk, Ltd.,
Marston Gate.